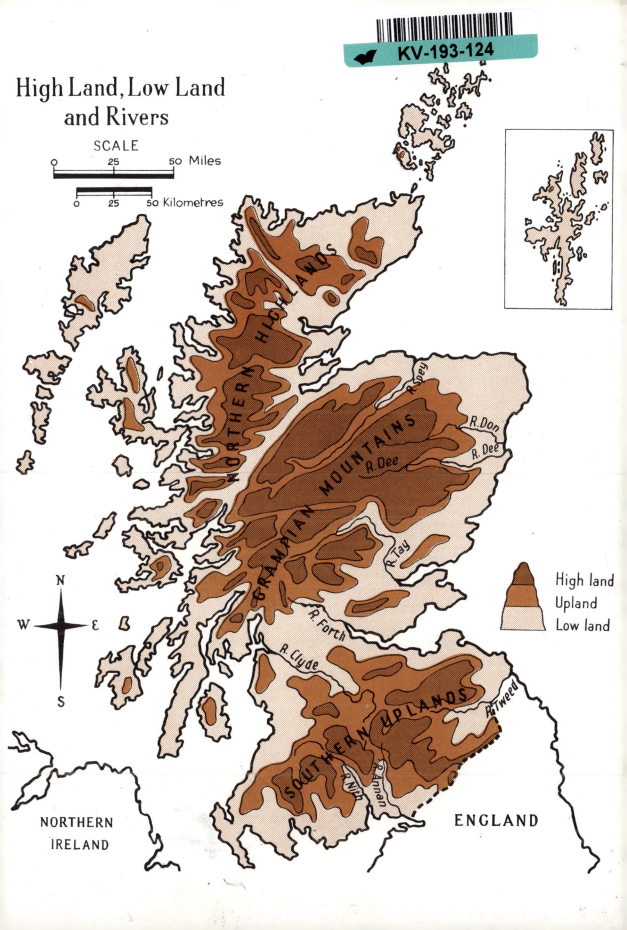

High Land, Low Land
and Rivers

SCALE

0 25 50 Miles

0 25 50 Kilometres

NORTHERN HIGHLANDS

GRAMPIAN MOUNTAINS

R. Spey

R. Don

R. Dee

R. Dee

R. Tay

R. Forth

R. Clyde

SOUTHERN UPLANDS

R. Tweed

R. Nith

R. Annan

NORTHERN
IRELAND

ENGLAND

High land
Upland
Low land

N
W   E
S

LOOKING AT GEOGRAPHY 5
General editor: R. J. Unstead

Looking at Scotland

JOHN M. WRIGHT

A and C Black London

Looking at Geography

The publishers are grateful to the following for permission to reproduce photographs:
Aberdeen Fish Market 48a; Aerofilms Ltd 69a; Bruce Armstrong 78c; W. A. Baxter &
Sons Ltd 49b; Blackwood Morton & Sons Ltd 22b; British Aluminium Company Ltd 20b;
BBC 75b; British European Airways 70b; The British Jute Trade Federal Council 22a;
British Petroleum Company Ltd 21, 29a; British Steel Corporation 17a; British Tourist
Authority 7a, 8b, 30a, 31a, 39b, 40b, 47a, 57a, 61a, 62c, 66b; Vincent Brown 1, 5a, 25b,
42a, 59b; Camera Press 55a; Captain John Carter and the North Eastern Press 54a;
J. Allan Cash 9a, 59a; Crown Copyright: Central Office of Information 62a; Cunard
Steamship Company 18b; The Distillers Company Ltd 44a; Donside Paper Company
Ltd 23; Farming News 6b, 28b, 32a, 36b and c, 37b, 38b, 39a, 47b; Forestry Commis-
sion 71, 72a, 73a and b, 74b; The Harris Tweed Association Ltd 60b; Eric Hosking
41a, 67c; Lyle & Scott Ltd 37c; A. D. S. Macpherson 6a, 28a, 30b, 52a, 53a and b;
Nair-Williamson Ltd 24b; National Association of Scottish Woollen Manufacturers 38a,
46b; National Coal Board 15c; North Eastern Press 4; North of Scotland Hydro-Electric
Board 75a, 76a; J. Peterson 63a, 66a, 67a; Planair 27; Andrew Paton 45b; W. Ralston Ltd
24a; Rootes Motors Scotland Ltd 20a; Jonathan Rutland cover a; Scotsman Publications
Ltd 7b, 9b, 17b, 26b, 65a, 74a; Scottish Agricultural Industries Ltd 35a and b, 36a;
Scottish Tourist Board 8a, 25a, 26a, 31b, 41c, 42b, 43a and b, 45a, 47c, 48b, 50a and b,
55b, 58b, 62b, 64, 77, 78a and b; Singer Manufacturing Company Ltd 18a; James R.
Smith & Son 16; United Kingdom Atomic Energy Authority 60a; Upper Clyde Shipbuilders Ltd cover b, 3, 19a and b; Valentine & Sons Ltd 49a; Agripress Publicity Ltd 34a.

The drawings are by Cyril Deakins and Geoffrey Whittam. The diagram on page 10 is by
D. B. Spink, as are the maps on pages 56, 72 and 76. The remaining maps are by Cyril
Webber. The maps on pages 14, 72 and 76 are based on ones originally drawn for the
BBC. The drawings on page 56 are based on ones originally drawn for the Herring
Industry Board. The drawing on page 57, from Torry Advisory Note No. 50 published
by H.M.S.O., and the maps on page 12 are reproduced by permission of the Controller
of Her Majesty's Stationery Office.

ISBN 0 7136 1158 8
THIRD EDITION 1971 REPRINTED 1974
© 1971 A. & C. BLACK LTD 4, 5 and 6 SOHO SQUARE
LONDON W1V 6AD
PRINTED IN GREAT BRITAIN BY
J. W. ARROWSMITH LTD., BRISTOL

CONTENTS

About this book 4

About this book

Scotland is a land of contrasts: in the north are barren mountain ranges, in the south are gently rolling hills. Between the north and south are the lowlands, where there is fertile farmland and large cities with many factories.

In this book you will read about these different parts of Scotland, and of the work of the people who live there. In the cities and towns they work at shipbuilding, engineering, coalmining and textile making. In the country they live by farming or – in more remote areas – by planting the bare mountain sides with trees, or building huge dams to make hydro-electricity. Around the coast are many fishermen. In the middle of the North Sea, men are drilling for oil.

Most of this book is about the people who live on the mainland of Scotland, but it also describes the life of the people who live on the islands of Orkney and Shetland.

The Highlands near Nedd village, Sutherland

1 What Scotland looks like

A bird's eye view

Look at the map on the back cover of this book. It shows what Scotland would look like if we could look down on it from an aeroplane on a very clear day. The patches of light green represent land which is a little above sea level. Different shades of brown are used to show higher ground. The highest mountains are easily picked out as they are printed in the darkest shade of brown.

The map shows that Scotland is a long narrow country, deeply cut into by firths, or estuaries, on the east coast. Along the west coast, which is fringed by more than five hundred islands, there are many sea lochs, which give the coastline a jagged appearance on the map.

Although Scotland is generally mountainous, it can be divided into three main areas:

1 the Southern Uplands
2 the Central Lowlands
3 the Highlands

The Lowther Hills

The Southern Uplands

Imagine that a line is drawn across the map from Girvan to Dunbar (see page 37). The part of the country southwards of that line, (towards the Scotland-England boundary), is called the Southern Uplands. This area is mainly hilly, but the hills are not very high. Two of the highest peaks are Broad Law and Hart Fell. Most of the hills are rounded and grass-covered to the top. The Moorfoot, the Lammermuir, the Lowther and the Cheviot Hills are in this area.

The River Tweed flows eastwards through a lovely, broad, fertile valley. On the northern shore of the Solway Firth is a wide, cultivated coastal plain, cut by the rivers Annan, Nith and Dee.

Standing on the north shore of the Solway Firth on a clear day, you can easily see the mountains of Cumberland and the Isle of Man in the distance. In places the waters of the Firth recede more than 1·5 kilometres at low tide and then it is possible to explore the small off-shore islands.

The rolling countryside is well wooded and the narrow roads twist and turn every few hundred metres. The farmers and village people who live here take a great pride in their homes and paint the outside walls white, or with a bright colour. These gay-looking houses give the impression that the people of this area are prosperous and contented.

British Friesian cow

6

The road bridge across the Firth of Tay

The Central Lowlands

Between the line drawn from Dunbar to Girvan, and another straight line from Stonehaven to Helensburgh on the Firth of Clyde, lie the Central Lowlands. Of Scotland's five million people, about four million live in this area. The Firth of Clyde, the Firth of Forth and the Firth of Tay are important waterways of the Central Lowlands. In the east and the west are wide coastal plains. Between the Firth of Forth and the Firth of Clyde is a plain only eighty kilometres wide. In recent years new towns have been planned and created, and continue to grow. Many new industries such as the manufacture of cameras, computers, typewriters, adding machines, tower cranes, transistors, plastics, and wire baskets and trolleys for supermarkets, employ more and more workers each year.

On the map of the Central Lowlands on page 14 you will find the Sidlaw Hills in Angus, the Ochil Hills in Fife, the Pentland Hills in Midlothian. Since they are easily climbed, they are popular with week-end hikers and ramblers. In the Central Lowlands there are rich farmlands as well as smoky industrial towns. Ugly slag hills and pit winding machinery show that there are coal mines.

7

Shipyards at Govan on the Clyde

Ben Nevis and Fort William

The Highlands

The Highlands of Scotland contain the highest mountain masses in Britain. Greatest of all is the towering, rugged peak of Ben Nevis, 1343 metres high. The steep rocky peaks of the Grampian Mountains form a barrier right across the country. The Cairngorms contain several summits over 1200 metres high. Best known of these are:- Cairngorm (1245 metres), Ben Macdhui (1309 metres), Cairntoul (1293 metres), and Braeriach (1295 metres).

In the south-west of Perthshire is a part of the Grampian Range which is frequently visited by tourists and holiday-makers. In the Trossachs, as this part of the country is called, nature has created a wonderful variety of beautiful scenery, with mountains, rivers, waterfalls, lochs and forests.

Loch Achray,
Trossachs

8

Highland cattle

Glen More, or the Great Glen, which divides the Highlands into two parts, stretches from Inverness to Fort William. In it are Loch Ness, Loch Oich and Loch Lochy. These three lochs have been joined by artificial waterways to form the Caledonian Canal. Fishing vessels and coasters of less than 600 tons use this short cut between the east and west coasts.

North of the Great Glen are the Northern Highlands. Here also the land is wild, rocky and mountainous. The roads are few and very narrow. It is possible to travel long distances without seeing a single house. Along the coast is a narrow plain where there are small farms. In the Black Isle, a promontory between the Moray Firth and the Cromarty Firth, the land is fertile and produces cereals.

In the far north, the shores of the Pentland Firth are very different from those of the Solway Firth. There are many sheltered bays with beautiful silvery sands, but there are also towering rocky cliffs which have caused the total loss of many ships driven against them in stormy weather. The north-west area of Sutherland is a land of bare mountains, lochs and moors, where very few people live.

In Caithness, however, the land is flat and green and there are many farm-houses. The farmers rear sheep and have a little arable land for growing potatoes, turnips and oats.

During winter, strong winds from the north bring Arctic-like blizzards to the two most northerly counties and it is not uncommon for farms and villages to be isolated for many days at a time. When the roads are filled with snow and impassable, the doctor at John o' Groats has to use a helicopter.

9

Glen Lednock dam

2 Weather and climate

Because the weather changes so often and so suddenly, it plays an important part in the life of the people of Scotland. Several times a day, weather forecasts are given on radio or on television. Daily newspapers, too, print a weather forecast and map. Long range forecasts are given for each month.

Many people need to know what the day's weather will be. All the year round the farmer likes to know what weather to expect, so that he can plan his day's work.

In spring, the market gardener must protect his young plants from night frosts. At lambing time, in February or March, a sudden snowfall can cause heavy losses to the shepherd who is not prepared for it. When harvest time comes, the farmer needs several days of fine dry weather to gather all his crops.

Mother listens to the forecast on washing day. At school the games teacher says: "The forecast is good today. We shall be able to go to the games field." Because the weather is so changeable, everyone is interested in it.

After studying the weather records over a great number of years, it is possible to say what the weather will generally be during the four seasons of the year. This is called the climate.

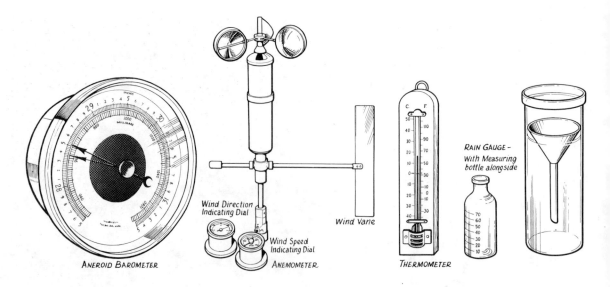

ANEROID BAROMETER
Wind Direction Indicating Dial
Wind Speed Indicating Dial
ANEMOMETER
Wind Vane
THERMOMETER
RAIN GAUGE – With Measuring bottle alongside

Instruments used in keeping weather records. The barometer measures air pressure, which is higher with dry air than wet air. The anemometer measures the strength of the wind.

Scotland is said to have a maritime climate because it is greatly influenced by the nearness of the sea. The usual winds from the south-west come across the Atlantic Ocean. These winds, which are warm and wet, bring plenty of rain at all seasons of the year.

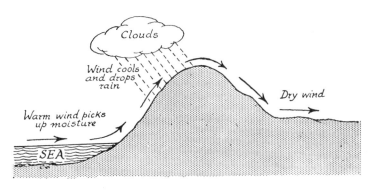

As the air is forced to rise, it cools and rain falls

most rain

moderate rain

least rain

Wind that blows
most frequently

SCALE
MILES   0   20   40   60
KILOMETRES 0   30   60

The high land of Scotland is in the north-west. That is where there is most rain

When warm wind strikes the mountains it is forced upwards. On reaching the cold upper air, the moisture in the wind changes to rain. Most of the rain falls on the western sides of the mountains. By the time the wind reaches the east coast it is drier, so the east of the country has much less rain than the west.

The heaviest rainfall occurs in the mountains north of the Firth of Clyde and in the Island of Skye. Here, more than 2000 millimetres of rain fall in a year. On the east coast about 750 millimetres is an average. The driest part of the country is the area that borders the Moray Firth.

The Gulf Stream is a current of warm water which drifts across the Atlantic Ocean from the Gulf of Mexico towards the British Isles. It has a strong influence on the climate of Scotland, for it warms the south-west winds. Because of it, the seas round the coasts do not freeze, even in the coldest weather. The Gulf Stream gradually loses itself in the icy waters of the Arctic Ocean.

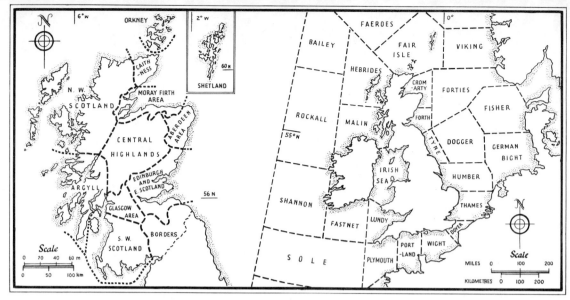

The weather forecast areas for Scotland, and for the seas around the British Isles

Between summer and winter temperatures there is not a big difference. During the year the south and west of Scotland are generally warmer in winter and cooler in summer. Inland places have greater differences in temperatures than places near the coast.

		AVERAGE TEMPERATURES		
		Winter	Summer	Difference
coastal	Aberdeen	2·4°C	13·2°C	10·8°C
	Wick	3·0°C	12·0°C	9·0°C
	Prestwick	4·2°C	14·2°C	10·0°C
	North Berwick	3·7°C	14·0°C	10·3°C
inland	Lairg	1·9°C	12·6°C	10·7°C
	Perth	2·6°C	14·5°C	11·9°C
	Peebles	2·3°C	13·4°C	11·1°C
	Braemar	0·6°C	12·4°C	11·8°C

Height above sea level also has an effect on temperature. As the land rises, the temperature falls. Peaks in the Grampians and the Cairngorms are snow-clad all winter, but most of the snow melts before the end of June. In some of the high corries in the Cairngorms snow is often found all the year round. A corrie is a bowl-shaped hollow in the mountains. When a corrie faces north, so that the snow in it is shaded from the summer sun by a shoulder of the mountain, the snow can lie all through the year.

Often in winter, icy winds from the north sweep over the country bringing frost and snow. Usually periods of extreme cold do not last very long, for after a time the south-west winds return, bringing to an end the snowball fights, the skating and the curling on frozen ponds.

January and February are the stormiest months of the year. Then strong winds are frequent. During the year, gale force winds are blowing in one day out of every ten.

12

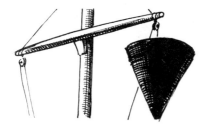

The "south cone" is hoisted by the coastguard as a gale warning. Long ago the coastguards' chief task was to catch smugglers, but today they are mainly concerned with saving lives

When a gale warning is given over the radio, small fishing vessels, herring drifters and seine net boats make for the nearest port. In the northern islands of Orkney and Shetland the gales are so severe that many of the houses have double windows for greater protection. Often during the winter the keepers in the lighthouse at Foula, off the Shetland coast, are cut off for three or four weeks at a time, because the supply boat cannot face the mountainous seas.

In summertime in the north of Scotland, the days are long and the nights are short. For three weeks before and after the longest day there is no real darkness at night. At midsummer in Shetland it is light enough to read a book out-of-doors at midnight. In winter, however, the night is long and the hours of daylight are few.

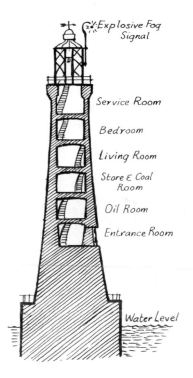

Lighthouses and lightships show a flashing light to warn ships about dangerous rocks or sandbanks

From March to September the northern hemisphere is tilted towards the sun

From September to March the northern hemisphere is tilted away from the sun

13

3 The Central Lowlands

Long long ago, before there were any people living on the earth, a great movement of the land took place. Right across Scotland, from east to west, two great cracks appeared in the earth's surface. Between the two openings the land began to sink.

When the earth movement had finished, the land between the cracks was well below the level of the land on either side. That is how the Central Lowlands were formed. Ice, snow, frost, wind and rain gradually wore away the great cliffs that were left on either side.

Look at the map on the opposite page. If two straight lines are drawn on the map, one from Stonehaven to Helensburgh, the other from Dunbar to Girvan, these lines will cut off the Central Lowlands from the rest of Scotland. The lines help you to understand where the great movement of land took place so long ago.

The Central Lowlands are the busy heart of Scotland. It is here that most of the Scottish people live and work. The prosperity of the Central Lowlands originally came from the coal and iron ore that were found together under the ground.

There is still plenty of coal, but little iron ore is left. Today most of the ore is imported from Spain, Algeria, or Sweden.

Coalfields

Coal is mined in five main areas, these are:

1   the Fife Coalfield
2   the Clackmannan and Stirling Coalfield
3   the Central or Lanarkshire Coalfield
4   the Lothians Coalfield
5   the Ayrshire Coalfield

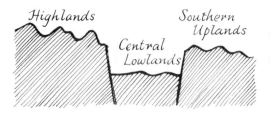

How the Central Lowlands were formed

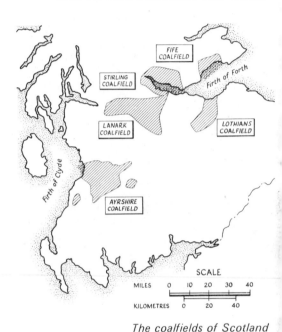

The coalfields of Scotland

Bilston Glen colliery, Lothians

Driving a new roadway underground in the Seafield Colliery, Fife

The Fife coalfield produces most coal. In all the coalfields, however, the coal seams near the surface have become exhausted. Some pits have been closed. To find good quality coal new pits have been opened and existing ones made much deeper. Some are over 900 metres deep. Machinery is used to cut the coal, load it and bring it to the surface.

At Longannet, on the northern shore of the Firth of Forth, is one of the most up-to-date collieries in the world. Four mines are joined together. All the coal from them is crushed and taken by conveyor belt to the huge furnaces which drive the turbines in the Longannet power station.

Glenrothes is a new town in Fife, a few kilometres north of Kirkcaldy. New factories are using the coal which is mined nearby.

Many thousands of men work in the coal mines. The machines that cut and load the coal do the heaviest work. But the miner at the coal face still has a hard job to do. His skill and experience produce the coal we need to keep our homes warm in winter.

One of the largest steelworks in Scotland, at Motherwell

4   Industries

Iron and steel

Many thousands of men work to make iron and steel. In producing steel or iron from the iron ore, there are two separate processes. First comes the process of smelting. The ore is placed in a blast furnace and heated until the iron in the ore melts. The molten iron is then poured into sand moulds and left to cool. This produces bars of pig iron.

The pig iron is sold to other firms who make it into steel. Again it is heated until it becomes liquid. The impurities are removed. New substances are added to make the steel tough and hard. Finally, it is pressed out in the shape of sheets, or bars, or ingots. Recently a huge new steel-making plant was built near Motherwell. At this plant both processes are completed under the same roof.

In Falkirk, the Carron iron works, which dates from 1759 and which is the oldest iron foundry in Britain, produces articles made of cast iron: baths, boilers, fireplaces and railings.

Other towns where the prosperity of the people depends almost entirely on iron and steel are Airdrie, Coatbridge, Motherwell and Wishaw in Lanarkshire, and Kilbirnie in Ayrshire.

17

Applying enamel powder to a bath at Falkirk

Engineering

Where there is steel-making there is, alongside it, engineering. Give an engineer a steel bar and he can make a nut and bolt or a screwdriver. With his skilful hands he can change steel tubes into a bicycle frame or a pump.

In the Central Lowlands there are two kinds of engineering – heavy and light. Railway engines, goods wagons, ships' boilers, large cranes and bulldozers are examples of heavy engineering. Sewing machines, electric motors, locks and metal chairs are made in light engineering workshops.

Assembling sewing machines

Scottish engineers have a world-wide reputation for first-class workmanship. Their products are sold in many different countries. Railway engines and coaches made in Glasgow are carrying passengers and goods in Argentina, Africa, Australia and India. Wire ropes made in Coatbridge are exported to many foreign countries.

Shipbuilding

Most of the steel produced in the Central Lowlands is used in the shipbuilding industry. The estuary of the River Clyde is one of the greatest shipbuilding areas in the world. Here, in 1812, Henry Bell built the "Comet" the first successful steamship. All sizes of vessels, from the "Queen Elizabeth 2" to a small coaster, are built on the Clyde. Many tradesmen are needed to make a ship. Platelayers, rivetters, welders, riggers, blacksmiths, carpenters, painters and electricians are some of them. Can you name any others?

Queen Elizabeth 2

Assembling one of the QE2's high pressure turbines

To the men who build it, and to the crew which sails it, a ship is a living thing. It must be humoured and taken care of. On the Clyde shipyards there is a great tradition of fine craftsmanship. The shipbuilders take a great pride and a personal interest in the ships they create.

After the ship has been launched, it is towed to a fitting-out basin, where the engines which will drive the propellers are fitted. As well as the engines, hundreds of other articles are required to furnish a large liner.

When the ship is ready to go to sea, it is like a small town. Chairs, tables, beds, wardrobes, baths, electric lights, blankets, sheets, tablecloths, carpets and linoleum are some of the furnishings needed. Making these articles gives work to thousands of people in Glasgow. When the fitting-out is completed, the ship is taken on trials before being handed over to her owners.

The Clyde is an ideal river for shipbuilding. For over thirty kilometres there is a wide, deep, sheltered channel, right into the heart of Glasgow. Dredgers keep the channel free from mud and sand. The important raw materials, coal and steel, are close at hand.

Dumbarton, Clydebank, Port Glasgow and Greenock are towns where most of the workers are engaged in shipbuilding. About one-third of all the ships built in the United Kingdom are launched from yards on Clydeside.

Govan Shipbuilders have now taken over the work previously done by the Upper Clyde Shipbuilders. John Brown's yard, which built the famous "Queen Elizabeth 2", is now producing oil rig platforms for use in the North Sea.

A passenger-cargo vessel on the building berth

Discing metal car bodies before painting

Extracting molten aluminium from the smelter at Fort William

Motor vehicles

A new industry in Scotland is the making of cars and lorries. These are mass-produced in large modern factories where thousands of vehicles can be assembled every week.

At Linwood near Paisley, Rootes make Hillman cars. In another adjoining factory they make steel bodies, squeezed into shape by huge presses. At Bathgate, the British Motor Corporation-Leyland group assemble many different types and sizes of commercial vehicles.

These factories give employment to many thousands of workers.

Aluminium

Bauxite is a reddish-brown clay from which a white substance called alumina is obtained. Aluminium is produced by smelting the alumina in electrically charged smelters.

At Invergordon in Ross and Cromarty, the British Aluminium Company has a giant smelter plant which produces 100,000 tonnes of the metal in a year. Large ore-carrying vessels bring alumina from Jamaica to a deep-water berth near the smelter.

Burntisland is a small port in Fife. Ships from Ghana unload cargoes of bauxite there. The alumina produced in Burntisland is used in paper making and water purification. It is also an important ingredient in toothpaste.

Aluminium is a strong, light metal with a great variety of uses. Pots, pans, kettles, caravans and motor-car engines are some of the articles made from aluminium.

North Sea oil

Have you ever heard of a roustabout? He is a man who works on an oil rig and keeps the drill going deeper and deeper in the search for oil. Recently oil has been discovered in several places under the bed of the North Sea. The drillers work from a floating platform anchored to the sea bed, or from an oil rig ship. The working platform is well out of the reach of the biggest waves. As a safety precaution, when the weather is really wild, the men are taken off the rig by helicopter.

It will be some time yet before the crude oil gets to a refinery. A pipe line is being laid from Cruden Bay on the Aberdeenshire coast to the refinery at Grangemouth, and an underwater section from Cruden Bay along the sea bed to the Forties oil field, about 170 kilometres away.

This new industry is bringing more work to the North East of Scotland. Not many men work on an oil rig but many more jobs have been created to keep the rigs going. A large fleet of helicopters is needed to ferry the crews to and from the drilling platforms. Special ships are required to keep the rigs supplied with food, pipes for lining the drilled holes and a large variety of drilling equipment.

John Brown's shipyard on the Clyde has been taken over by Marathon Shipbuilders who are building North Sea oil rigs. At Nigg Bay on the Cromarty Firth, about 1300 men are employed producing drilling platforms.

Perhaps when all the wells under the North Sea are flowing, oil from these wells will be able to supply all the petrol that the country needs.

Oil rig in position over the Forties oil field

A circular loom for weaving jute cloth

Carpet making in a Kilmarnock factory

Textiles

The prosperity of the inhabitants of Dundee depends to a great extent on the jute industry. Jute is imported from India and Pakistan. The fibres are obtained from the inner stem. From jute is made a coarse textile called *hessian*. This is used for making sacks, for packaging, and in upholstery. It is also used as a backing for rugs and linoleum.

Beautiful carpets, in a great variety of designs and sizes, are woven on large looms in factories in Glasgow, Kilmarnock and Ayr. Because they are made from wool, they are warm and soft under your feet. The bright colours, and the attractive designs, help to brighten our homes, as well as making them more comfortable. Scottish carpets are exported to all parts of the world.

Cotton thread for sewing is manufactured in the town of Paisley. In Dundee, Kirkcaldy and Dunfermline are factories where linen goods are woven. Linen threads are obtained from the fibres of the flax plant, grown in Germany, Belgium, France and Ireland. All over Scotland there are woollen mills making knitwear and woven fabrics.

Chemical Industries

Throughout Scotland there are many industries in which different substances are mixed together to give a final product quite unlike any of the original materials. As a rule expensive machinery is needed, and a highly trained chemist is in charge of the work.

At Aberdeen there is a large chemical works which produces cattle feed and fertilisers for the farmers in the north of Scotland. Cargoes of phosphates and sulphates from Morocco or from islands in the Pacific are landed at the harbour. These are the raw materials from which the fertilisers are made.

At Aberdeen harbour, too, are landed large cargoes of esparto grass from Spain and from Casablanca in North Africa. On the outskirts of the city are two very large paper mills, one on the River Dee and one on the River Don. In these mills the esparto grass becomes high-quality paper.

In Edinburgh there are large rubber factories where tyres, boots, gloves and balls are manufactured. The rubber comes from trees growing in Malaysia or Sumatra. At Leith hundreds of tonnes of artificial fertilisers are produced every week. Plastics and detergents are obtained from the crude oil at the Grangemouth refinery. In a factory at Irvine, in Ayrshire, nylon fibres are made.

On the north-west coast there are lovely beaches of fine silver sand, which is very good for making glass. Boatloads of the sand are taken to glass works in Glasgow where it is melted in furnaces and made into glass. Bottles, electric lamps and glass wool are made from it. The glass wool is packed round large boilers and helps to keep in the heat. In the far north, at Wick, a factory turns out tinted ornamental and table glassware. It is called "Caithness Glass."

At Stevenston, on the Ayrshire coast, there is a large factory for making explosives. The commonest form of explosive is dynamite. It is used for making detonators, in tunnelling, and for blasting in quarries. It is exported to all parts of the world. The factory where the explosives are made covers a large area of ground, because it consists of a number of small buildings well separated from each other. The reason for this is that if there was an accidental explosion, only a small section of the factory would be damaged.

This photograph of a paper mill near Aberdeen shows raw materials stacked on the right and finished bales of paper leaving the factory by lorry

Working on the wiring of a telephone cable

Cushioned vinyl floor covering is being made in this factory at Kirkcaldy

Plastics

Plastic pens, coats, water tanks, sandals, bags, chairs – there is no end to the number of articles made of some kind of plastic material. Four main varieties of plastics are made in Scotland.

Nylon is a tough hard wearing fibre used for clothing, tyrecord, ropes, nets and belting. **Expanded polystyrene** combines lightness with strength. It is made into ceiling tiles and bulb bowls and is used for packing delicate equipment such as cameras, radios and scientific instruments. **Polythene** bags are everywhere. A tougher variety is made into bottles, bottle tops, combs, toys and tableware. **Urethane** foam slabs are now widely used in upholstery instead of flock and hair.

Some of the places where plastics are made are Aberdeen, Dumfries, Falkirk, Glasgow, Grangemouth and Penicuick.

Electronics

Many of today's scientific marvels such as your transistor radio, your television set, your mono or stereo record player, or the computers that guided the astronauts to the moon, would not have been possible without the science of electronics. It is a very special branch of the electrical industry and is concerned with making an electric current pass through a vacuum or gas.

Radio valves or television tubes are electronic devices. Some transistor valves are very tiny and require great deftness and delicacy of touch to assemble them. Much of this work is done by highly skilled women.

There are factories producing electronic equipment in Falkirk, Glenrothes, Kirkcaldy, Dundee, Motherwell and Edinburgh.

24

Edinburgh Castle and Princes Street

5 Cities and towns of the Central Lowlands

Edinburgh

Edinburgh is the capital of Scotland. It is a lovely city, with many fine buildings and open spaces. Princes Street, the main thoroughfare, is considered one of the finest streets in Europe. One side of the street consists of tall buildings with many shops. Along the other side stretches a series of well-kept gardens.

Standing guard over the city is the ancient castle. It is perched on the top of a huge volcanic rock, 120 metres high. Visitors like to wander through the rooms and look at the old weapons and suits of armour. St. Margaret's Chapel is within the castle walls. This is the oldest chapel in Scotland, built more than 800 years ago for Queen Margaret of Scotland.

From the Castle to the Palace of Holyrood is a distance of just over $1\frac{1}{2}$ kilometres, or one mile. This is called the Royal Mile because so often in olden days Scottish kings and queens travelled this road from the Palace to the Castle. St. Giles is the best-known of the city's churches. On the outskirts of the city is a large zoo. A great variety of animals, birds and reptiles are kept there.

Holyrood Palace

The military tattoo at the Edinburgh Festival

Every year, in the month of August, an International Festival of Music and Drama is held in the capital. For the three weeks of the festival, famous orchestras, musicians and singers give concerts and recitals. Operas and plays are performed by selected companies. From many overseas countries thousands of tourists visit the city to see and hear the performances.

One of the most attractive items is the military tattoo, in which kilted pipers, regimental brass bands and noisy mock battles thrill the crowds of watchers.

Because Edinburgh is the capital city, the chief Scottish Law Courts are there. It is also an important centre for banking and insurance. The city's population of almost half a million is spread over a wide area and, although factory chimneys are not obvious, there are many important industries. Printing, publishing and brewing employ many people. Many engineering works specialise in making electrical and electronic equipment.

Leith docks

Leith

Leith, the seaport of Edinburgh, is the largest port on the east coast. Although it was at one time a separate town, it is now a part of the capital. Ships from many continental countries unload cargoes at Leith docks. Iron ore from Sweden, bacon from Denmark, esparto grass from Spain, and wheat from Canada, are some of the imports. Near the docks are the largest flour mills in the country. Flour from these mills is sent to bakers in many parts of Scotland. Shipbuilding is another important industry.

26

New buildings and road development in central Glasgow

Glasgow

Glasgow is the largest city in Scotland. In Great Britain, only London and Birmingham are larger, and around one million people live in this huge city. Glasgow owes its size and its importance to its favourable position at the head of a wide, navigable estuary. Quite near Glasgow is the Central or Lanarkshire coalfield. Coal is still the chief source of power, both for smelting the iron and for driving the machinery in the factories and workshops.

Glasgow imports great quantities of food and raw materials from all over the world. From its docks are exported daily a wide variety of products. Here are some: sewing machines, adding machines, tweeds, whisky, seed potatoes, cattle and locomotives.

During the 18th and 19th centuries, the growing industries in Glasgow and its neighbouring towns needed many workers. People from the Highlands and Islands crowded into the big city where work was plentiful and wages high. This is one of the reasons why so few people now live in the Highlands of Scotland.

All kinds of things are made in or near Glasgow: shoes, woollen goods, furniture, jam, cigarettes, clothes, chocolates and field glasses.

At Greenock, where James Watt was born, there are large factories for refining sugar. Syrup and treacle are also made from sugar.

27

Dundee from the north end of the modern Tay road bridge

Dundee

Dundee is a seaport at the mouth of the River Tay. Tall factory chimneys can be seen everywhere. Forty jute mills employ about 18,000 workers, many of them women. Before 1930 Dundee's prosperity depended almost entirely on the jute trade. Although it is still the town's chief industry, the trade has shrunk. Research chemists are constantly trying to find new uses for the material. In the shiny, new factories a wide variety of articles is made: cash registers, clocks, watches and electrical goods. Shipbuilding also employs many men. Large cargo vessels are built in the Dundee shipyards.

Along the north bank of the River Tay, between Perth and Dundee, stretches the Carse of Gowrie. It is a sheltered, fertile part of the river valley where soft fruits, mainly raspberries, are grown for making jam.

Perth

As it is the centre of a rich agricultural district, Perth has become a market town where farmers can sell their produce and buy what they require for their farms. Important cattle sales are held there. The animals are sold by auction to the highest bidder. Buyers come from many overseas countries to bid for the best animals. There is also a dye works and a whisky distillery.

Important cattle auctions are held at Perth

28

Crude oil from the Middle East and South America is brought by tanker to the new ocean terminal at Finnart on Loch Long

Stirling

Stirling, on the River Forth, is a town that is steeped in history. On the out-skirts of the town, the battle of Bannockburn was fought in 1314. In early times Stirling was important in guarding the road to the Highlands. Its castle, on a towering rock, stood guard over the river where it was most easily crossed. Today it is the market town of the district. Farmers' tools, ploughs, harrows, scythes and reaping machines are made. There is also a carpet-making industry.

In Loch Long, a deep sea loch on the Firth of Clyde, there is a pier used only by oil tankers. The crude oil, which the tankers bring to Scotland from the oil wells in the Middle East, is pumped out of the vessels and stored in huge tanks built into the hillside. From these tanks the oil travels through pipelines to Grangemouth, a seaport on the Firth of Forth. Here, in a large refinery, the crude oil is changed into diesel oil, lubricating oil, paraffin and petrol.

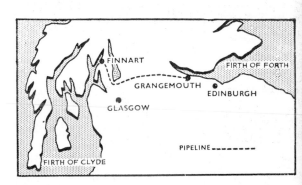

Kilmarnock

Kilmarnock is an industrial town in the north of Ayrshire where there is a carpet weaving industry and large engineering works.

29

Scotland's new towns

There are five new towns in Scotland, all of them in the Central Lowlands.

The largest is **East Kilbride** where many Glasgow families have gone to live and work. One firm has a world-wide trade in machinery that changes salt sea-water into fresh water. The equipment is called a desalination plant. In another factory, telephones are made. Rolls Royce make engines for the latest jet aeroplanes.

The youngest of the five towns is **Irvine** in Ayrshire. The old small burghs of Irvine and Killwinning, along with some nearby villages, have been grouped together to make the new town. A great variety of goods is manufactured. Fork-lift trucks, chemicals, golf clubs, ball bearings, nylon fibres and glassware are some of them.

Livingston near Edinburgh is the smallest, but it is growing as quickly as houses and factories can be built. The Cameron Iron Works employ many skilled engineers. Asbestos sheets and pipes are manufactured. In the making of clothing, knitwear, shortbread and locks, many women find employment.

The people of **Cumbernauld** are very proud of the fact that architects from many different countries visit their town to study the way it has been planned and built. Motor cars have been kept away from the shopping areas and from the children's play areas. There are plenty of jobs in Cumbernauld. Computers, floor coverings, window frames, meters, clothing and footwear are made there.

In the lovely town of **Glenrothes** in Fife there are over forty new industries employing more than 6,000 workers. Several factories produce electronic equipment. Transistor radios, telephones, toys, wire baskets, trolleys and petrol pumps are manufactured there.

Children in a special play area at Cumbernauld

30

Holiday towns

Hotels and boarding houses are really part of a great industry. Now that nearly all workers get two or three weeks' holiday in the summertime, with pay, millions of people every summer look for somewhere to go for their holidays. Those who cater for the tourist or holiday-maker must earn enough in the summer months to keep themselves for the rest of the year.

Ayr is on the west coast. It has hotels and boarding houses where holiday-makers stay in the summertime. Robert Burns, Scotland's national poet, was born near Ayr.

In the Firth of Clyde there are many holiday towns which attract great numbers from the industrial area of the Central Lowlands. These towns can offer the visitors everything they require for a happy holiday – warm sunny weather, fine sea air, golfing, boating and swimming. Rothesay, Helensburgh, Dunoon, Largs, Brodick, Ardrossan, Saltcoats, Troon and Girvan, as well as Ayr, are all within easy reach of Glasgow.

On the east coast there are beautiful sandy beaches, the air is brisker and more invigorating, but the temperature is usually a little lower. Stonehaven, Carnoustie, St. Andrews, North Berwick and Dunbar attract large numbers of visitors each year.

At the seaside resorts you can meet the weather-beaten fishermen, dressed in thick woollen jerseys and long rubber boots, mending nets or getting lobster creels ready.

The beach at Carnoustie

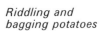
Riddling and bagging potatoes

6 Agriculture in the Central Lowlands

Oats

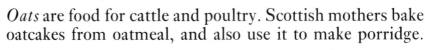

Although the Central Lowlands is considered the main industrial part of Scotland, farming is also very important there. In Angus, Fife, Perthshire, the Lothians and Ayrshire, there are broad fertile farms. All over Scotland, oats, barley, turnips, potatoes and grass grow well. Turnips, however, do not grow very well in the west.

Oats are food for cattle and poultry. Scottish mothers bake oatcakes from oatmeal, and also use it to make porridge.

Barley is used in the making of beer and whisky. It is also good cattle food. "Barley Beef" is the name given to cattle that have been reared indoors mainly on barley.

Barley

Turnips provide winter feeding for sheep and cattle.

Potatoes grow very well in Scotland. Seed potatoes are exported to many foreign countries. Only the very best are accepted as seed. When a farmer wishes to sell his crop for seed, an inspector examines his potatoes while they are still growing. Only if they are true to variety and free from any disease is the farmer permitted to sell them as seed. They are much dearer than the ones you have for dinner.

Turnips

Two kinds of potatoes are grown – Early and Main Crop. Potatoes grow well in the good soil and favourable climate of Ayrshire; the early potatoes are ready in June. Main crop potatoes are the ones which keep over the winter till next year's earlies are ready. They are harvested in October.

For storing during the winter, the potatoes are heaped in shallow pits or clamps shaped like this ∧. The rain runs easily off the sides. On top of the potatoes is a layer of straw to keep out the frost. Earth is heaped over the straw. In places the straw sticks out at the top for ventilation. Even the keenest frost will not reach the potatoes in a well-made pit.

Making a potato clamp

Grass

Apples

Grass is very important to the dairy farmer and the cattle breeder. As droughts are rare, the grass keeps green and sweet all through the summer months. This helps to produce plenty of milk from the cows and fat bullocks for the butcher. Good grass does not grow by accident. The farmer carefully chooses the right kind of seed to give him rich pasture and good hay.

Raspberries

Blackcurrants

In the Clyde valley much of the land is used for growing fruit. Apples, plums, strawberries and tomatoes (under glass) grow well. In Carluke, a small town in Lanarkshire, the fruit is used to make jam.

In Angus, between the Grampian Mountains and the Sidlaw Hills, lies a wide fertile plain called Strathmore. Wheat and fruit grow well. Forfar is the market town for the district. Great quantities of seed potatoes are grown. There is also plenty of rich pasture to fatten the large herds of beef cattle.

Strawberries

Pruning

Combine harvesters at work in Angus

One of the few areas where wheat will grow and ripen in Scotland is in the three Lothian counties. Scottish-grown wheat is a soft variety. Before the flour reaches the baker it is mixed with harder wheat from Canada or Australia. The seed is sown in early autumn. When the plant is a few centimetres high, the winter frosts shrivel up the leaf. The roots go to sleep.

At the first rays of warm spring sunshine, the roots are ready to send up a new strong shoot which grows quickly. In autumn the golden grain is ready for the reaping machine, or for the combine harvester.

Farmers know that they cannot grow the same crops on the same fields every year. Different plants take different foods from the soil. To keep the cultivated land in good condition, the farmer changes the crops in his fields each year. In the Lothians the farmers use the six-year rotation which is shown below.

A six-year rotation of crops in one field

	Field A	Field B	Field C	Field D	Field E	Field F
1st year	oats	potatoes	wheat	roots	barley	grass
2nd year	potatoes	wheat	roots	barley	grass	oats
3rd year	wheat	roots	barley	grass	oats	potatoes
4th year	roots	barley	grass	oats	potatoes	wheat
5th year	barley	grass	oats	potatoes	wheat	roots
6th year	grass	oats	potatoes	wheat	roots	barley

Hens on deep litter

The dairy farms of the Central Lowlands produce plenty of milk for the people in the towns. Some of the milk is made into butter and cheese. The farmers also rear bullocks, sheep and pigs for the butcher's shop and grow potatoes for the greengrocer. Market gardeners grow the other vegetables which the greengrocer sells.

On a mixed farm the farmer's wife usually looks after the hens. What she earns by selling the eggs and poultry is regarded as her "pin" money. She may keep a few dozen laying hens in a grass field. The birds have plenty of freedom to roam around and are said to be "on the range". One drawback to having hens on the range is that they often lay away from their nests and the eggs are difficult to find.

Most eggs come from large poultry farms, where the hens are kept either in a battery or on deep litter inside a large poultry house. Bright lamps give them artificial sunlight. Birds reared on deep litter get plenty of exercise scratching about in a thick layer of peat moss, but they never get out of their shed. Battery hens are kept in wire cages but they do not seem to suffer from the lack of exercise, for they still lay five or six eggs each week.

Hens in a battery

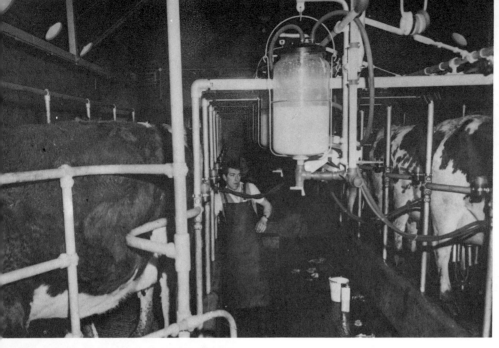

A milking shed

An Ayrshire cow

Ayrshire is the farming area which supplies the millions of workers living in Glasgow and the neighbouring towns. The county has given its name to a famous breed of milk cow – Ayrshires, beautiful brown and white animals which give a good supply of rich creamy milk. The breed is popular all over the country.

The Milk Marketing Board is responsible for collecting the milk from the farms and bringing it to the large towns. The dairies receive their milk from the Board. By this arrangement the farmer receives a guaranteed price for all the milk which his cows produce.

In many large dairies the milk is pasteurised before it is sold. It is heated until it is very hot, but not boiling. This kills any harmful germs which may be in it. Then it is cooled and bottled, ready for delivery.

In Ayrshire the Milk Marketing Board sends its extra milk to factories where it is made into butter or cheese.

Milk passing through a cooler before being bottled

36

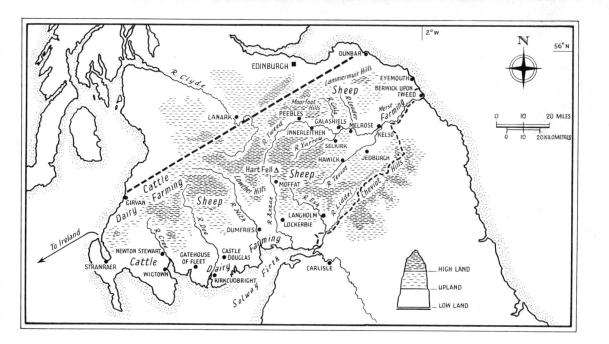

7   The Southern Uplands

Cheviot and Tweed

In hilly country where the soil and the slope of the land are unsuitable for arable and dairy-farming, sheep are valuable animals. They thrive best on dry pastures. In the east, the grass covered slopes of the Cheviot Hills support large numbers of sheep which are kept mainly for their wool. The most popular breed is the "Cheviot," because it has a heavy fleece of fine wool.

In the valley of the River Tweed is a very important woollen industry. The Tweed has given its name to a tough, hard-wearing cloth of good quality. At Galashiels, Hawick, Selkirk and Peebles there are many factories which specialise in high-quality woollen goods. Tweeds, blankets, hosiery and knitwear are made. Tweed is used to make suits, sports jackets, overcoats, skirts and dresses. Rugs, scarves, stoles and ties are also made. Knitwear is made on knitting machines, which turn out jumpers, cardigans, pullovers, dresses, socks and stockings.

RIGHT   *Stitching together the sleeves and body of a jumper made in a Hawick factory*

BELOW   *A Cheviot sheep*

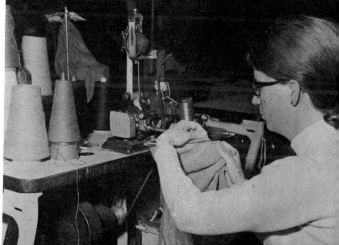

Dealing with a consignment of new wool on the sorting bench in a Scottish mill

Although there is a good supply of wool from local sheep, more is imported from Australia, New Zealand and South Africa to satisfy the demand for the high-class cloth woven in this area. The tweed towns have a large export trade to America and Canada.

The lower valley of the Tweed is a rich, agricultural district called the Merse. The chief cereal grown is oats, but barley and some wheat are also grown. A good supply of turnips is grown as winter fodder for the sheep. At Kelso, buyers from many overseas countries come to the annual ram sales held in October.

The Western Plains

There are few important industries in the western side of the Southern Uplands. The largest town is Dumfries, where 28,000 people live. "Queen of the South," Dumfries is an attractive town on the banks of the River Nith. It is a market centre for the farmers in the district. There are also tweed mills, a factory where rubber footwear and golf balls are made, and another where condensed milk is produced.

At Annan, on the Solway Firth, is the Chapelcross Atomic Power Station.

There are no large towns in the Western Plains. Sanquhar, Lockerbie, Moffat, Castle Douglas, Kirkcudbright and Stranraer are market towns where the farmers come to sell their produce and to buy seed, agricultural implements, stores and everyday goods for their homes. Langholm, a small town on the River Esk, has some of the most famous woollen mills in Scotland.

Kelso ram sales. The man in the white coat is the auctioneer

38

A champion Galloway bull

In this part of the country the river valleys are called dales. In the lower parts of the dales, the arable land grows oats and root crops. The grassy slopes of the hills provide pasture for large flocks of sheep.

Galloway is the name given to the area covered by the two counties of Wigtown and Kirkcudbright. Most of the farms are devoted to dairy farming and the milk is sent on lorries to the Newcastle district and to the big cities of Lancashire. Much of the extra milk is sent to creameries in the market towns where it is made into butter and cheese. The skimmed milk left over from the butter-making is used for feeding pigs. This helps them to fatten quickly for the market. Many Galloway cattle are bred to provide high-quality meat.

From Stranraer there is a regular steamer service to Larne in Northern Ireland. This is the shortest route between the two countries. The Caledonian Princess, a fast modern car ferry, does the crossing in just over two hours.

Rivers, forests, hills, moorlands and grassy and craggy slopes give a variety of scenery which is the charm of the Border Country. For centuries before England and Scotland were united, this countryside was the scene of many raids and fights between raiding bands, whose chief way of making a living was by stealing sheep and cattle from across the border.

At Melrose, Dryburgh, Jedburgh and Kelso you can still see the ruins of what were once lovely abbeys. Sir Walter Scott, the famous novelist, lived at Abbotsford, near Melrose. The lush and beautiful "Scott Country" inspired many of his stories.

Jedburgh Abbey

39

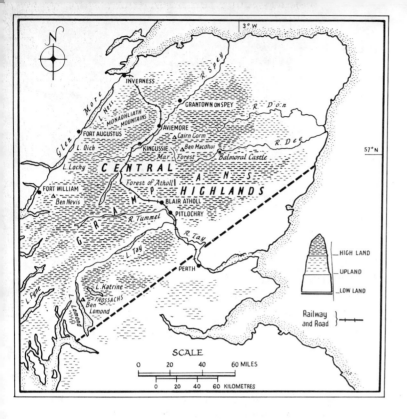

8   The Central Highlands

The Grampian Mountains

The Grampian Mountains stretch right across the centre of Scotland from the north-east coastal plain, through the counties of Aberdeen, Perth and Inverness, to the west coast of Argyll. This is wild and desolate country. It is the land of the red deer, the grouse, the mountain hare, the eagle, hawk, raven and the wild cat. The mountains are rugged and strewn with boulders. Where there is a little soil, heather, moss and grass grow. In August and September, when the heather is in bloom, the hills are a glorious purple.

Large herds of the wild red deer roam through the heart of the mountains in search of food. They are shy, timid creatures, constantly alert to danger. It is very difficult to get near them unless you are a clever stalker. The moors on which the deer live are called "deer

Devil's Elbow, Grampians

40

forests," but now there are few trees left. A few years ago some reindeer from Lapland were brought to the Cairngorms. There are now about sixty of these attractive animals in the herd. If you walk along the mountain tracks near Aviemore, you may be lucky enough to see some of them.

The landowners who have deer forests on their estates employ gamekeepers to look after the animals and birds which wealthy sportsmen come and shoot at certain seasons of the year. A gamekeeper has a healthy, interesting job, though it is a lonely life living in a cottage in the heart of the hills. His children have long distances to walk to and from school.

In the course of his duties a game-keeper may walk over 30 kilometres in a day, but he is never in a hurry. He gets to know the mountains, the animals and the birds, as well as you know your own home. He must keep the land free of vermin – animals or birds which would harm the game. His gun and his dog are his constant companions. In the springtime he burns large areas of old, straggly heather. Baby grouse do not thrive well in old heather and burning it encourages new shoots to spring up.

During the shooting season the game-keeper guides the sportsmen to the places where the game are to be found. If they are stalking the deer, then he makes sure that only the older animals are shot. The flesh of deer is called venison; it looks rather like beef, but is drier and has a different flavour.

Reindeer in the Cairngorms

Pheasant   *Red Grouse*

41   *Grouse shooting*

A farm between Carrbridge and Inverness

All over the mountains there are springs of clear, ice-cold water bubbling out of the ground. As the water trickles downwards, different springs come together to form a burn. Further on, the burns join up to form a stream or a river, which flows through the main valley. There are, too, many lochs and bogs amongst the hills.

Where the river valleys begin to broaden out, it is often possible to cultivate some of the land. The small farms are called crofts and the farmer who works one is a crofter.

Usually, the crofter keeps a milking cow, some sheep, and hens. He grows oats, potatoes, turnips, and grass for hay. If his croft is very small he must also have another job to do. He may work as a forester or on a bigger farm not too far away; almost certainly he will be taken on as a beater during the shooting season. At best, the crofter finds it difficult to make a living.

Near the Trossachs, at the southern edge of the Grampians, there are small towns whose chief industry is looking after the tourists who come from all over the world to see the magnificent scenery. Such towns are: Dunblane, Callander, Aberfoyle,

Studying the route on the Dukes Road, Perthshire

42

Carrbridge

Bridge of Allan, Crieff and Comrie. Their boarding houses and hotels are usually full up during the summer months. For hikers and cyclists there are several Youth Hostels. There is plenty for the visitors to do. They can climb mountains, take bus tours through some of Scotland's loveliest scenery, play golf or tennis, fish for trout in the burns, or simply laze about in the warm sunshine.

Across the heart of the mountains there are very few roads. To get to Inverness from Perth there is only one direct route, which is followed both by the road and the railway. The route follows the valleys of the Tay and the Garry, through Dunkeld, Pitlochry and Blair Atholl. From there it passes over barren heather-clad moors where there are few houses to be seen. After climbing to 460 metres the road gradually drops into the valley of the Spey. As the valley broadens, farms take the place of bare moorlands. The hillsides are clothed with pine woods. In Speyside, the road and the railway pass through Kingussie, Aviemore and Carrbridge before reaching Inverness.

Strath Spey

The River Spey rises in the mountains between Loch Laggan and Loch Lochy. Between the river valley and Glen More lie the Monadliath Mountains. This area of land is a high, heather-covered, deserted plateau.

The Spey is a sparkling and swift-flowing river. Anglers from all over the country come to Speyside for their holidays, hoping to catch large salmon. Angling for salmon is a sport requiring great skill and patience. To grass a "twenty-pounder" (about 9 kilogrammes in weight) is a fitting reward.

Fishing in the Spey

Speyside is famous as the natural home of the whisky-making industry. Scotch whisky is well known throughout the world, and it is one thing that can be successfully made only in Scotland. Attempts to make "whisky" in other parts of the world have not produced the same result. No one is certain of the reason for this. Some experts think that it is the combination of the climate and the water which gives Scotch whisky its distinctive flavour.

Whisky is made in a distillery, which is a large building like a factory. From fermented barley a weak solution of alcohol is obtained. The solution is placed in a large copper still which may hold 18,000 litres at a time. The long narrow coiled tube that forms the neck of the still passes through a tank of cold water.

When the liquid in the still is heated, the alcohol in the mixture boils at a much lower temperature than the water. As the alcohol vapour passes through the cold tubing of the still, it condenses and becomes liquid again. This process of distilling is repeated a few times until only pure alcohol is left. The liquid is then left to mature in old oaken casks for a period of from three to fifteen years.

Mountaineering equipment. The steel pegs, called pitons, are driven into the rock, and the rope runs through them

Rothes, Aberlour, Dufftown and Grantown are small towns in the heart of the whisky-producing area. Millions of litres of whisky are made every year. Scotch whisky is exported to many countries, especially to America, Canada, Western Europe and Japan.

Climbing and ski-ing

The Highlands of Scotland form a great natural playground for those who are interested in outdoor sports, such as camping, climbing, ski-ing and

44

orienteering. For the climbers, June, July, August and September are the best months. By that time of the year the winter snows have melted and the weather is most likely to be favourable.

But even on the finest days the weather can change very rapidly. If a mist comes down, the landscape is blotted out and a single false step may lead to disaster. When in-experienced climbers are caught in the mist, the safest course is to wait for the air to clear. Experienced mountaineers and rock climbers can find plenty of areas where they can test their skill and agility. No part of Scotland is far away from the mountains and many young men and women from the industrial towns enjoy the pure air and the solitude of the hills.

Ben Nevis, because it is the highest mountain, is an attraction for many. It is within easy reach of Fort William, a small town on the Caledonian Canal which caters for climbers. Another popular area is the Cairngorms which can be reached from Aviemore on Speyside, or from Braemar on Deeside.

In recent years ski-ing has become a very popular winter pastime. For about six weeks at the beginning of the year, there is always snow above 600 metres. If the weather has been severe the snow lies much lower down. The upper slopes of the Cairngorms give splendid conditions for ski-ing, because of their height. The building of ski tows and chair lifts on well-known slopes at Aviemore, Glenshee and Glencoe has done much to make the sport very popular. When there is plenty of snow, thousands of people of all ages enjoy an invigorating and strenuous week-end on a pair of skis.

The chairlift at Aviemore

9 The North-East Coastal Plain

From the county of Kincardine the coastal plain stretches round the north-east counties of Scotland to Inverness. The plain is crossed by the rivers South Esk, North Esk, Dee, Don, Deveron, Spey and Findhorn.

Farming is important in the north-east coastal plain. Oats, barley, potatoes, turnips and carrots are grown. In the counties of Moray and Nairn, wheat grows well, because the climate is mild and the soil is fertile. Large flocks of sheep provide the wool for many mills scattered throughout this part of the country.

Many of the small county towns and villages have a mill which specialises in a particular type of woollen material, such as gloves, stockings, blankets, flannel, light tweed for suits, or heavy tweed for overcoats. These goods must be of first-class quality to compete with the mills of the Tweed valley and Yorkshire.

Examining the finished material in a woollen mill

46

Aberdeen-Angus cattle, black with wide shoulders and short legs, are considered to be the finest of all the beef cattle. At the annual Perth bull sales the prize-winning animals sell for thousands of pounds. Usually they are bought by cattle ranchers from North or South America. Shorthorns and Herefords are also reared, but not in large numbers.

Many farmers buy "store cattle" from Ireland to fatten up for the butcher. These "stores" are bought when about one year old and fed for a year to eighteen months. Then they are ready to be sold as fat cattle.

The people who live in the villages in the valley of the River Dee cater for summer visitors. Many holiday-makers enjoy the bracing air and the beautiful mountain scenery. Every summer the Queen and her family spend six weeks in Balmoral Castle, which is situated on a lovely part of the river.

It was at Braemar that the Earl of Mar raised the standard for Bonnie Prince Charlie in 1745. Every year in early September members of the Royal Family attend the Braemar Gathering to see the athletes and dancers competing at the Highland Games. Throwing the hammer, putting the weight, tossing the caber, wrestling, highland dancing and bagpipe playing are the events which attract large crowds.

Balmoral Castle

A prize-winning Aberdeen-Angus bull

Throwing the hammer at the Braemar Games

Aberdeen

Aberdeen, with a population of 186,000 is the third largest city in Scotland, and the largest town in the north-east. It is often called the Granite City because most of its buildings are made of grey granite – the stone which is found locally. In the sunshine the granite glitters and sparkles as the tiny pieces of mica in the stone reflect the light. Marischal College, one of the university colleges, is the largest granite building in Great Britain.

Two of Aberdeen's chief industries are connected with fishing and granite. Because the vast granite quarry no longer yields top quality stone, much of the granite that is worked in the city is imported from Scandinavia.

Granite is an immensely hard stone. Blocks of it are sent to many parts of the country for monuments, and as foundations for piers and bridges.

In Aberdeen there are paper mills, tweed mills and one large factory where flax canvas hosepipes are made. These hosepipes are sprayed with rubber on the inside to make them waterproof. They are bought by shipping firms and by fire brigades in many different countries. In the shipbuilding yards, trawlers, tugs and small cargo vessels are built. Some engineering firms make plantation machinery, which is exported to the tea estates of Assam and Ceylon and to the rubber estates in Malaysia.

Marischal College, Aberdeen

48

The harbour at Fraserburgh

The small towns

Round the coast are a number of small towns where fishing is an important industry. At Peterhead, Fraserburgh, Macduff, Buckie and Lossiemouth, there are fleets of modern dual-purpose vessels fishing for sprats, herring, white fish, shrimps or prawns all the year round. A dual-purpose boat can catch fish on the sea bed with a seine net, or do mid-water trawling. Many of these vessels operate in the seas off the west coast, sometimes berthing in Mallaig for the weekend while the men travel home by crew bus.

At Peterhead there is an engineering works where all sizes of twist drills are made. There is also a large canning factory employing about 700 workers. During the summer herring season, they cook and can herrings.

At Fraserburgh there is a tool factory employing hundreds of men from the surrounding district. They make tools driven by compressed air, for use in road-making and mining. A large modern canning factory employs about 400 workers who process and can herrings and kippers.

Fochabers is a prosperous village in Moray, not far from the mouth of the River Spey. Here there is a large canning factory which employs 500 workers at the busy season. The firm makes typical Scottish foods, such as haggis, roast grouse, roast pheasant, scotch broth and cock-a-leekie soup, as well as delicious jams and sauces.

49

Checking random cans as they come off the production line at Fochabers

Elgin is the county town of Morayshire. It is in the centre of a rich agricultural district, where wheat and barley are the main crops. There is a large woollen mill where vicuna cloth is made. The raw material for the cloth is the fine silky wool of the vicuna, a small wild animal like the llama, which is found only on the borders of Chile and Peru. As the vicuna is hunted and killed for the sake of its wool, supplies of vicuna wool are scarce. Its wool is the finest that can be obtained. Most of it is exported to America.

Inverness, which is at the northern end of the Caledonian Canal, is sometimes called the Capital of the Highlands. All the roads and railways to the north pass through the town. Woollen goods are manufactured and whisky is made here.

During the summer many thousands of tourists pass through the city, most of them to visit Loch Ness, hoping to catch a glimpse of the "Loch Ness Monster."

Inverness and the River Ness

10   The fishing industry

All round the coasts of Scotland, in towns, villages and hamlets, are men who earn their living by their skill at catching fish. These men were born within sound of the waves. They follow the sea because their fathers and grandfathers were fishermen before them. Over the years they have gained a·wealth of knowledge about the effects of the wind, the weather and the tides on the fish they hope to catch.

Fishing may be divided, roughly, into two kinds:
1   inshore
2   deep sea

Salmon fishing

The most profitable form of inshore fishing is salmon fishing. Every year the salmon come in large numbers to spawn in the swift, clean waters of the Scottish rivers. Many men are employed in catching them. The fishing season lasts from March until August, but it varies slightly in different areas. In the estuaries of the rivers the ring net is used to trap the fish entering the river. Along sandy beaches near the rivers, stake nets are used.

To catch the salmon by "ringing," a long net is piled into a flat-bottomed boat, a salmon cobble. The cobble is rowed across the river to the other bank and back again, while the net falls into the water. By pulling the two ends of the net together, a ring of netting is formed, which traps the fish lying within it.

This operation is repeated many times during the day, but, by law, the river must be left free of nets from noon on Saturday until 6 a.m. the following Monday. During this period the fish can get up-stream to spawn, or to provide sport for the anglers further up the river.

Catching salmon by "ringing"

51

Using stake nets in the tidal waters of the Nith

Stake nets are so called because the nets are attached to long poles, or stakes, which are driven into the sands at the water's edge when the tide is out. At high tide, only the tips of the stakes can be seen. The fishermen visit the nets twice a day, when the tide is half out, and remove the trapped salmon by means of a net with a long handle. These stake nets are set out at regular intervals on the coast, near the mouths of salmon rivers. From experience the fishermen know the best places to erect their nets.

Because there is never enough salmon to satisfy the demand, it is the most expensive of all fish. The best known salmon rivers are the Tweed, Tay, Dee, Don, Spey, Findhorn, and the Solway Firth. The value of the salmon, grilse and trout caught every year is well over one million pounds.

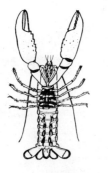

Inshore fishing

Some inshore fishermen, in places where the coast line is rocky, catch fish by means of lines with baited hooks fixed to them. Setting off in their boat, they may lay up to three kilometres of lines with a hook every two metres. They hope to catch cod, haddock, catfish, or plaice. (When the catfish reaches the fishmonger's shop it is called "rock turbot".)

The inshore fishermen have a difficult and dangerous job in their small, motor-driven boats. When the sea is rough they dare not leave the shore.

A crab and a lobster (the undersides)

The final stage in the making of a lobster pot. It is coated with tar to preserve it in the water

Many inshore fishermen earn a living by setting traps for lobsters and crabs. The traps or creels are wooden box-shaped frames, covered with wide-mesh netting. The lobster enters the trap by a narrow tunnel of netting. Once inside, it cannot get out again. Each trap is attached by a rope to a buoy, so that it can easily be found and pulled up again.

In the Hebrides, on the north and west coasts, and in the Orkney Islands, some of the fishing is done by crofters during the spring and autumn months. The Highland Industrial Development Board has helped many fishermen from these areas to get their own boats and to work their vessels all the year round. On the east coast they catch lobsters, crabs and prawns at all seasons of the year. The best grounds are found near Peterhead, Fraserburgh, Boddam, Johnshaven, Anstruther, North Berwick and Eyemouth.

Lobsters and crabs go bad very quickly after they are dead. They can, however, live for a long time out of the water. When carefully packed in boxes, with ice, they will survive the long journey from the outer islands to London.

At Thurso, Peterhead, Inverbervie and Berwick-on-Tweed, there are factories where crabs and lobsters are processed. They are cooked, packed, and deep frozen. Even the shells are not wasted. They are ground into tiny pieces and added to poultry food. The lime in the shells is good for hens.

53

Lobster fishing on the north coast of Scotland

A seine net boat at Fraserburgh

A seine net boat is about the same size as a small trawler. It may be built of iron or of wood. Many fishermen still prefer a wooden fishing vessel. At many of the small fishing ports there are yards where these boats are made by builders with long experience of their craft.

A seine net is used for catching fish which live on or near the bed of the sea. When the skipper has decided where he is to cast his net, he places a marker buoy in the water. To the buoy he fixes several coils of strong rope which are attached to one end of the net. He steers his boat over a triangular course paying out a long length of rope – then the net – and then more rope, as he sails back to his marker buoy.

The seine net is like a bag of netting with two long wings tapering to a narrow cod-end in the centre. Weights take the net down to the bottom of the sea. The buoy is then taken aboard when the boat gets back to it, and the two ends of the rope are put together in the winch. While the winch is winding in the ropes, the boat moves slowly forward. The action of winding in the ropes gradually pulls the wings of the net together so that the fish lying between them are directed into the cod-end.

Because they are small, seine net boats do not go to distant fishing grounds. They usually remain at sea for three or four days. Many return to port every day. The fish is landed while still very fresh, so it fetches good prices.

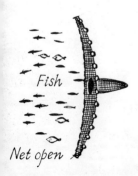

Net open

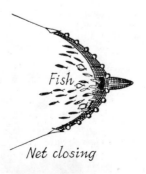

Net closing

Net closed

As the net is drawn towards the boat, the fish are trapped in the cod end

A twin trawl net bulging with cod

Seine net boats sail from Macduff and Lossiemouth to fish in the Moray Firth area. Other east coast ports are Fraserburgh, Buckie, Peterhead, Stonehaven, Montrose, Gourdon, Arbroath, Anstruther, Pittenweem, Dunbar, Port Seton and Eyemouth. In the north there is Serabster and in the west are Kinlochbervie, Ullapool, Mallaig, Oban, Ayr and Girvan.

Deep sea fishing

This is mostly confined to trawling in near and middle distance waters by trawlers and seine netters.

Aberdeen is the chief trawler port and its fish market, which is 270 metres long, handles about 300 tonnes of white fish every day. A fleet of trawlers which fish the near and middle-distance fishing grounds, operates from the port. The trawlers bring in halibut, cod, haddock, sole, plaice, ling and turbot, which are called white fish. Because the vessels do not go for long trips, the fish is very fresh and of good quality. Packed with ice in boxes, it is sent by train and lorry daily to Glasgow, London, Manchester, Birmingham, and other large cities and towns.

When fish are exported to far-away countries such as Africa, America, or Mediterranean countries, they are quick-frozen. This means that they are put into a cold store which quickly reduces the temperature of the fish to thirty degrees below zero centigrade. The fish are kept at this temperature in special railway vans, or in ships' holds, throughout their journey.

Packing fish with ice at Aberdeen

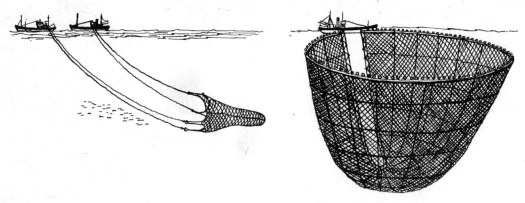

Midwater trawling   Purse seining

The herring is a very important fish to many Scottish fishermen. Four methods are used to catch the herring. These are by midwater trawl net, purse seine net, ring net and drift net.

The most popular method is by midwater trawl operated by boats working in pairs. This type of net may cost £1500.

Purse seining is the most recent method used to catch herring. The boats work singly or in pairs. When working in pairs, one boat acts as guide. Having located a shoal of herring it remains above the shoal while the other casts the net. As the net is hauled in, it forms a huge bag and the herring in it are forced to the surface. They are then scooped on board or drawn through a suction pump. A net of this type may cost £18,000.

Ring net fishing is carried out by boats working in pairs in calm water such as the Clyde area, the Firth of Forth and the sea lochs of the west coast. A ring net may cost £1800.

The traditional method of catching herring is by drift net. The boat that fished only for herring was called a drifter. A "fleet" of 60 to 80 nets was cast into the sea one after the other, pulled down by a heavy leader rope and kept upright by cork floats and large buoys. As boat and nets drifted with the tide, the herrings were caught in the net by their gills. Today only a handful of drifters remain. In time these also will disappear.

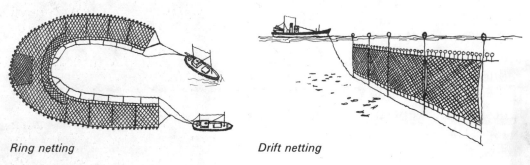

Ring netting   Drift netting

One reason for the decline of the herring drifter is that it is more costly to run than a dual-purpose vessel. No machine has yet been devised to haul in drift nets. All the nets must be hauled aboard by hand and the fish shaken out of them on to the deck. This is very hard exhausting work and extra men are needed to crew the drifter.

Over 800,000 crans of herring are loaded every year. A cran is a measure by volume (four baskets equal one cran) and, depending on size, may contain from 700 to 2500 fish; 5·6 crans make one tonne.

Only a very small amount of the herring catch is sold as fresh herrings in the fishmonger's shop. Most of the fish are preserved in some way so that they can be eaten months after they were taken from the sea. Herring may be preserved by quick freezing, by canning, by smoking or by klondyking. Klondyked herring are packed in boxes with ice and a little salt on top and are exported to Denmark, Norway, Germany and Holland.

To make kippers, the herring are split open, soaked in brine with a little dye, and then smoked in a kiln over a fire of hardwood chips. Most kippering firms now use a mechanical kiln called a Torry kiln where the temperature and the amount of smoke is electrically controlled.

Many other workers depend on the fishermen for their daily work. There are the men who build and repair the fishing boats, the net makers, the makers of ice, rope, sails and boxes, and the merchants who supply the boats with food. Can you name any others?

In many fishing ports there is at least one fish meal factory. To it are sent daily all the fish that have not been sold in the market. The fish are steamed in huge boilers, which reduces them to a pulpy mass. This mass is then dried by hot air until it becomes a grey powder called fish meal. It is used in the making of special foods for animals. Fish oil is also produced at these factories. It may be used in making paint and varnish.

A Torry kiln for smoking fish

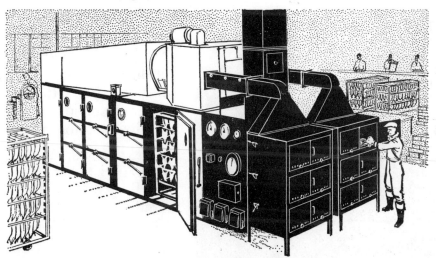

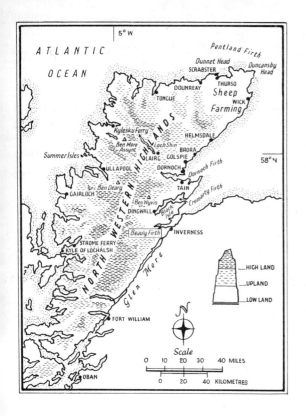

11 The Northern Highlands

North of the Great Glen, the mountains are, for the most part, bare, barren, rugged and inhospitable. Apart from aluminium works at Fort William and Foyers, an occasional wool mill or distillery, and a new mill for making paper pulp and paper at Corpach near Fort William, there is very little industry and the few people earn a living by agriculture, forestry and fishing. The building of oil rig platforms at Nigg Bay on the Cromarty Firth has brought hundreds of jobs to the area. Many people think that the discovery of oil wells in the North Sea will bring new life and prosperity to this part of the country.

Except for the narrow coastal plain, the country is almost uninhabited. In the burns and rivers there are plenty of brown trout and salmon. The golden eagle nests high on the mountain ledges. On the high wind-swept moors, the antlered stag roams freely.

There are few roads across this part of the country, and most of these are very narrow, for they are rarely wide enough to allow two cars to pass abreast. Every few hundred metres the road is widened for a short distance so that vehicles can pass each other.

On the west coast the mountains seem to tumble right into the sea. Very little land can be cultivated and the farmer has to be both fisherman and crofter in order to earn a living. When the boys and girls are ready to leave school, there is no work for them in the neighbourhood so that they must find a job in some other part of the country. Many west coast highlanders speak Gaelic when they are at home. They are a kindly, hospitable people, who are very proud of their ancient Scottish heritage.

Liathach and Ben Eighe, Glen Torridon

58

Oban. Notice how the hills slope down almost to the water's edge

A glance at the map on page 58 will show you that along the west coast there are many fiords or sea lochs. These bite deeply into the coast and make travel from north to south very difficult. At some of them, Loch Linnhe and Loch Carron, there are regular ferryboats. To cross most of them, however, means a journey of perhaps 15 kilometres along one bank and 15 kilometres back again along the other bank. Ardnamurchan, a peninsula in Argyllshire, is the most westerly point in the mainland of Britain.

Oban is the largest town in the Western Highlands. It is an attractive seaside town on the Firth of Lorne, which caters mainly for summer visitors. From Oban, supply-steamers sail regularly for the Western Islands. Near Ballachulish on Loch Linnhe there are slate quarries which produce good hard slates for the builders.

Not far from Ullapool, limestone quarries produce much of the lime that is used by North of Scotland farmers.

On the eastern side of the Northern Highlands there is a wider coastal plain, and more land can be cultivated. The Black Isle, which is neither black nor an island, is fertile and has a mild climate. Oats, barley and root crops grow well.

59

Ferry boat which crosses Loch Carron

The Dounreay atomic power station, Caithness

In Glen More, and near the town of Beauly, cattle rearing is important. The bright yellow buildings of the Great Glen cattle ranch catch the eyes of the travellers in the region. Large flocks of sheep graze on the hills, and more than 10,000 lambs are sold every autumn at the Thurso lamb sales. About the end of the 18th century, many farmers, with their families, emigrated to Canada and the U.S.A. That is one of the reasons why so few people now live in the area.

A railway line runs north from Inverness to Wick and Thurso. Along the eastern coast there are the small towns of Dingwall, Dornoch, Brora, Helmsdale, Wick and Thurso. Each has a small fishing fleet. Near Thurso is a large atomic power station, called Dounreay. At Brora is the only coal mine in the North of Scotland. It is a small pit, owned by the miners who work it, which produces enough coal for the district.

12   The Hebrides

Off the west coast of Scotland there are about 500 islands. They form two groups called the Outer Hebrides and the Inner Hebrides. In the Outer Hebrides the largest islands are Lewis and Harris, North Uist, South Uist, Benbecula and Barra. The largest of the Inner Hebrides are Skye, Rum, Eigg, Mull, Tyree, Colonsay, Jura and Islay.

Harris tweed is hand-woven by the islanders at home

60

The harbour at Stornoway

About one hundred of the islands are inhabited. They are the homeland of a proud
independent people who speak Gaelic. Their
names begin with Mac – Macdonald, Mac-
kenzie, Macleod, Maclean. Because there are
no industries apart from agriculture, fishing
and weaving, young people have to leave the
islands to look for work.

LEWIS is the largest of the islands. The
southern part of it is called HARRIS. Twenty-
seven thousand people live on the island.
Stornoway, the largest town, is an important
herring port. Good catches of herring are
obtained in the Minch.

Harris has given its name to a famous kind of
tweed that is woven on the island. It is
rough, warm, hard-wearing material used to
make men's suits, sports jackets and overcoats, as well as women's skirts and topcoats.
Harris tweed is exported in large quantities
to America. The weaving of the cloth is
largely a cottage industry. Many islanders
have looms in their own homes and the
whole family helps to produce the tweed.
Large flocks of sheep on the island provide
the wool for weaving.

SKYE is the second largest island and probably
the best known of them all. At one point it is
quite near the mainland and a ferryboat
large enough to carry motor-cars connects
Kyle of Lochalsh on the mainland, and
Kyleakin on the island.

Crofting and fishing are the main occupations
of the people. Because Skye is famous in song
and story, many thousands of tourists visit it
each year. The island is very mountainous.
The Cuillins, which rise to over 900 metres,
attract many mountaineers. Dunvegan Castle
in the north-west is the home of the MacLeod
of MacLeods.

The Hebrides

A modern croft in North Skye. The house has mains electricity, water and a telephone. Notice the pile of peat on the left

Iona cathedral

Digging peat on Harris

MULL is another of the Hebrides which attracts many visitors. The rugged beauty of the mountains, the unhurried ways of life, the pure clear air, and the smell of peat fires, are things that city dwellers find most refreshing. In the north-east corner of the island is Tobermory Bay. Here some of the treasure galleons of the Spanish Armada were wrecked in 1588.

Off the south-west corner of the island lies the small island of IONA. It was on this island that St. Columba built his monastery from which he and many other monks took Christianity to the rest of Scotland and Northern England. In recent years young men and women from Scottish churches have spent their holidays on the island, where they have laboured to rebuild the church and monastery.

Life in the smaller islands of the Hebrides has changed little over the years. The pace is slow and leisurely. All goods to and from the mainland must be carried by boat and MacBrayne's steamers from Oban give a regular service. Roads on the islands are often poor, but modern houses and bungalows with electric light are now replacing the primitive stone cottages with their paraffin lamps. Peat, cut from the moss and dried in the sun, is the common fuel.

13   Orkney and Shetland

The many islands which make up the counties of Orkney and Shetland stretch northwards from the mainland of Scotland for nearly 270 kilometres. They are windswept and treeless, but the clear, pure air, and the great variety of scenery, give them an unusual beauty. In summer, when there is scarcely any darkness, the moors are carpeted with wild flowers; the towering cliffs are nesting places for thousands of sea birds; the quiet, sandy bays are dotted with tiny sailing boats; and the small tidy fields are green with corn and grass.

To understand the people of Orkney and Shetland it is well to remember that these islands belonged to Norway until 1470, when King James III of Scotland married Margaret, daughter of Christian I, King of the Scandinavian countries. He received Orkney and Shetland as a marriage dowry. The islanders still retain their Norwegian laws and customs, and to this day they think of themselves as Norse rather than Scottish.

Orkney

The Orkney Islands – there are about 70 of them – stretch 80 kilometres northwards from the coast of Caithness. Although only 10 kilometres of the Pentland Firth separate Caithness and South Ronaldsay, they are 10 kilometres of the roughest water round the British Isles. Here the currents of the Atlantic Ocean, meeting those from the North Sea, give boat passengers an unhappy time.

Gannets nesting on the cliffs of the island of Ness, which is a bird sanctuary

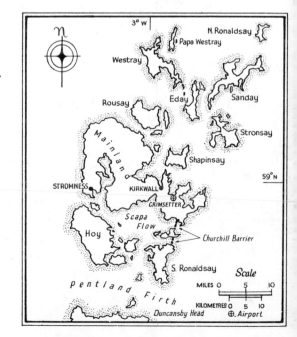

The Islands of Orkney

A street in Kirkwall

MAINLAND, the largest island of the group, contains the only two towns of any size in Orkney – Kirkwall and Stromness. Westray, Sanday, Rousay, Stronsay, South Ronaldsay and Hoy are some of the larger islands. Between Mainland, Hoy and South Ronaldsay there is a large area of sheltered, deep water called Scapa Flow.

Except for the Island of Hoy, which is hilly, most of the islands are fairly flat and the soil is fertile. The population of 20,000 are mainly farmers or crofters. Oats, potatoes, turnips and grass are the regular crops.

Large numbers of Cheviot sheep and cattle are bred in Orkney and in recent years poultry farming has become very important, millions of eggs being produced every year.

There are valuable lobster fisheries round the coasts. At Kirkwall the lobsters are packed in ice, shipped to Aberdeen, and finish the journey to London by train. Large hotels and passenger liners buy great numbers of these shellfish.

Kirkwall is the chief town of the Orkneys and one of the oldest Royal Burghs in Scotland. Visitors find the narrow, winding streets attractive and interesting. Its fine harbour is a busy place, as the town is the trading and shopping centre for all the islands in Orkney. The varied produce of the farmers' fields and poultry houses come to Kirkwall, from where they are sent to Aberdeen by steamer.

The people of Kirkwall are very proud of St. Magnus Cathedral which is over 800 years old.

Shetland   If you board the fine modern steamer *St. Clair* at Aberdeen harbour, fourteen hours' sailing will take you to Lerwick, the capital of Shetland. If you do not like the sea trip, an aeroplane can do the journey in less than two hours. The distance between the two towns is 290 kilometres.

64

The harbour at Lerwick, the capital of Shetland

In summertime the harbour at Lerwick presents a busy scene as the herring boats arrive with their catches. The prosperity of the islands depends very much on the results of the herring season. Big catches mean plenty of work for the curers, the coopers and the fish meal factory. Most of the catch is cured and exported to the Continent.

Lerwick is the only town of any size in the islands. About 6000 people live there. It is built right on the sea front and, indeed, some of the houses stand in a metre of water.

The Shetland Islands consist of about one hundred islands, of which twenty are inhabited. Fewer than 100 people live on some of the smaller islands. Largest of them all is the Mainland which is 87 kilometres long and 34 kilometres across at its widest point.

The land is rough and hilly. The coastline varies from steep unscaleable cliffs to beautiful sandy beaches. Rona's Hill, in the north of the Mainland, rises to a height of 450 metres.

Sumburgh Head is the most southerly point of the Mainland. About 110 kilometres north is Muckle Flugga, the most northerly part of Great Britain.

The Shetland Islands

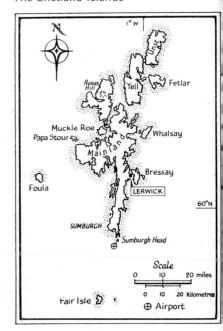

65

Lambs being landed in the Shetland Islands, for shipment to Aberdeen

Of the other islands, the largest are Yell, Unst, Fetlar, Whalsay, Bressay, Foula and Fair Isle. About 20,000 people live in the Shetlands. Most of them earn a living by cultivating their small crofts. Oats, potatoes, turnips and cabbages are grown.

Fishing is an important and prosperous industry. Most of the catch is processed and exported to America.

A Shetland knitter

Shetland is famous for its hand-knitted garments. Shawls, scarves, gloves, pullovers, cardigans, berets, helmets, stockings and underwear are knitted by hand. The Shetland style of knitting is quite different from the style in any other part of the country. There is a co-operative association which sells the articles for the knitters and makes sure that they get a fair price for their work. Much of the knitting is done during the winter when work on the croft is at a standstill.

The wool that gives the quality of lightness with warmth, comes from the Shetland sheep. This animal is small, lean, tough and hardy. It is out-of-doors all the year round and must forage for its food on the heather-covered hills. In summer the wool is plucked by hand from the animal when it is ready to shed its winter coat. The carding and spinning of the wool is still done in a few homes, but most of it is sent to mills in Brora, Inverness and Keith where the work is done much more quickly.

In Fair Isle the women colour their own wool with dyes made from lichens and mosses. From Unst come the famous Shetland shawls which mothers all over the country buy for their babies.

Shetland ponies

Foula is the most westerly of the islands. It is only five kilometres long and four kilometres wide, yet about a hundred people live there. Fishing and sheep rearing are the main occupations. Its cliffs are the highest vertical cliffs in Britain, and, over the years, the waves have pounded great caves out of the solid rocks.

Fetlar is sometimes called the garden of Shetland. Many Shetland ponies are bred here and sent to different parts of the country as children's pets. They are small, sturdy, affectionate animals which are allowed to roam at will over the hills and moors to fend for themselves.

Shetland is a wonderful place for birds. They nest in their thousands on the rocky cliffs and moor-covered hills. Here are the names of some of the sea birds which nest in Shetland and which are not commonly seen on the mainland of Britain: Great Skua, Arctic Skua, Red-throated Diver, Fulmar Petrel, Storm Petrel, Whimbrel, Tern and Shag. The island of Noss, and Hermaness, a part of Unst, are bird sanctuaries, where the parent birds can rear their young in perfect safety.

In a land where the tang of the sea air is everywhere, and where no part of the land is more than five kilometres from the ocean, it is not surprising that many Shetland men choose the sea as their career.

A Fulmar defending its nest

67

14 Travel and transport

By road

If you look at a road map of Scotland, you will see that the great network of roads in the south and in the centre gradually thins out towards the northern regions. But a road map does not give a complete picture of the road system, for it shows only the first class and second class roads. (The letter "A" represents first class, and "B" the second class roads.) In addition there is a vast number of narrow, less important roads, leading to the villages and hamlets which lie some distance from the great trunk roads. Parts of the trunk roads between Edinburgh, Glasgow, Perth, Stirling and Carlisle are gradually being replaced by motorways.

Although roadmen are constantly at work repairing and improving existing roads, by removing bad corners and by widening narrow roads, in many places the roads are not good enough to carry all the traffic on them. With two new bridges, over the River Forth near Edinburgh and the River Tay at Dundee, road traffic on the East Coast route has been greatly speeded up. The new road bridge over the Forth is a superb example of the bridge builder's art and is one of the loveliest suspension bridges ever built.

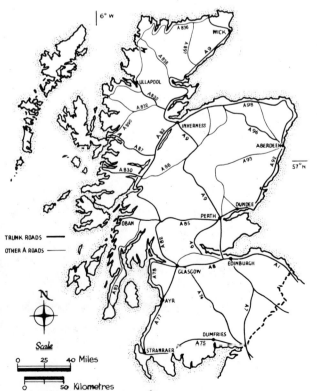

Most of the lorries on the roads carry regular supplies of food, raw materials for the factories, or finished goods from the factories.

By rail

By rail there are two routes from Scotland into England. The West Coast route, from Glasgow, follows the valley of the River Clyde and crosses the border near the village of Gretna at the head of the Solway Firth. The East Coast route, from Edinburgh, keeps to the coastline and reaches the border at Berwick. Travelling north from Edinburgh the track is carried across the Forth and Tay estuaries by the Forth Bridge and the Tay Bridge, two wonderful examples of bridge building.

The main roads

68

The road and railway bridges across the Firth of Forth

From the Tay the line runs north to Aberdeen and then to Inverness by way of Keith and Elgin. From Inverness to Thurso, where the East Coast route ends, is a further six hours' journey. This stretch of railway runs through some of the finest mountain and coastal scenery in the whole of Scotland. A little north of Inverness a branch line goes westwards through the Northern Highlands to Kyle of Lochalsh. Apart from this line, and the line from Glasgow to Oban, there are no railways in the north-west of Scotland.

Diesel rail cars have been introduced on many routes and diesel electric locomotives have taken the place of steam engines. Soon the railway from Glasgow to London will be all electric. The new trains on this line will be able to travel at over 160 km/h.

The railways still carry a huge volume of goods traffic. For the transport of fish and meat there are special refrigerated wagons which keep the food at a low temperature during the journey. There are also specially designed wagons for carrying timber, coal, furniture and cattle. An ever-increasing quantity of exports and imports are being carried in large, metal, box-shaped containers. These are lifted by crane from the ship's hold to the railway bogey. The contents cannot be touched until the container is unlocked at its destination.

The main railway lines

69

People who send goods by rail are charged according to the weight of the goods and the distance they have to travel. The cost of transport affects the price of most of the things you buy. Edinburgh is near a coalfield, but Inverness is far from one, so coal is much dearer in Inverness than in Edinburgh. Some people think that British Rail should charge by weight alone, as the Post Office does. What do you think?

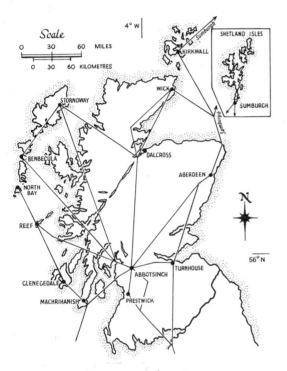

Airports and air routes

By air

The air route map shows that Glasgow's airport, Abbotsinch, is the most important airport in Scotland. It is like the hub of a wheel from which spokes radiate to all the other airports in Scotland.

Because air travel is so speedy, it is very useful in case of illness or any other emergency. People living in the islands of the Hebrides, Orkney, or Shetland who become dangerously ill, can quickly be flown to the nearest hospital on the mainland. An air ambulance is stationed at Abbotsinch for emergency cases.

Airfields, with their long, concrete runways, require a great deal of space, so they are generally some distance from the towns which they serve. The time taken in travelling from an airfield to the city centre often adds greatly to the total time of a journey. In the future, inter-city flights will probably be by helicopters, which will land right in the centre of the cities.

Prestwick, near Ayr, is the largest airport in Scotland and the only one which has runways long enough for the large trans-Atlantic jet-engined aircraft. During foggy days in winter it is often the only airfield in Britain free from fog.

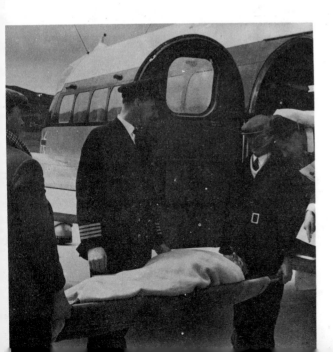

A patient is carried into an air ambulance at Barra

70

Forest on Drummond Hill, Perthshire

15   The work of the Forestry Commission

If you look around your classroom you will see many things made of wood: pencils, rulers, desks, cupboards, chairs, tables and floor boards. You could probably fill a page with the names of different articles for which wood is the raw material. Joiners, carpenters, cabinet makers and boxmakers are tradesmen who are constantly working with it. In order to keep up a steady supply of timber, foresters, lumberjacks and saw millers are steadily at work, growing, cutting down and sawing the trees.

There are two different varieties of timber – soft woods and hard woods. All the timber used in making a house, the rafters, beams, floors, doors and window frames, is soft wood. The furniture is made of hard wood.

Pine, spruce, larch and fir are the trees which yield soft wood. They grow quickly and thrive on rather poor soil. All of these trees are conifers, which means that the seeds grow in the form of cones. Except for the larch, they are also evergreens. Their leaves are needle shaped.

In Scotland the commonest hard woods are oak and beech. They grow much more slowly than the conifers and require a richer soil to nourish them. All the hardwood trees, which are deciduous, have broad leaves.

During the two world wars which have taken place this century, most of Scotland's trees were cut down. In times of war there are no ships to spare to import timber from other countries. The great quantities of timber needed every day had to come from our own forests. In fifteen minutes a lumberjack can cut down a tree which has taken 80 years to grow. By the end of the Second World War most of Scotland's hills and mountains, which had carried great forests, looked bare, torn, and deserted.

71

Planting young spruce trees

The Forestry Commission is a government department which is concerned with the welfare of the country's trees. When most of the older forests were cut down, the government decided that new ones must be planted. The Commission was given power to buy land from landowners and to establish forests.

Today there are 172 forests all over the country, covering more than 700,000 hectares of land. Most of the land is quite unsuitable for agriculture. It is mainly moorland, peat moss, or mountain-side, where the soil is of poor quality. When a little agricultural land is within the boundaries of the forest, it is let to the forest workers, who are allowed to work it as a small croft.

Most of the trees are grown from seed in four large tree nurseries near Elgin, Alloa, Newton Stewart and Dornoch. The seed comes from cones collected in Scotland, Europe, North America and Japan.

In its first year the young tree only grows about 150 millimetres high. At the end of its first year it is transplanted. When two years old it is 300 millimetres high and ready for its permanent home in the forest. The planting is done between the months of October and April.

Before the trees are put in, the ground is ploughed by a large forest plough drawn by a powerful tractor. The trees are planted on top of the ridges, and the hollows help to drain away the extra water.

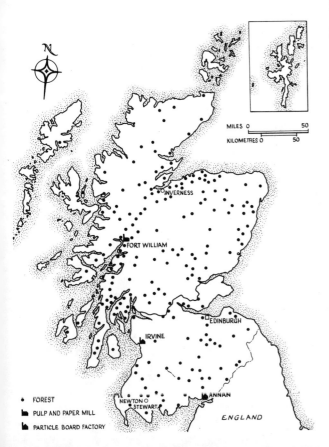

MILES 0   50

KILOMETRES 0   50

INVERNESS

FORT WILLIAM

EDINBURGH

IRVINE

NEWTON O
STEWART

ANNAN

ENGLAND

•   FOREST

▸   PULP AND PAPER MILL

▸   PARTICLE BOARD FACTORY

Forests and pulp and paper mills

72

Felling trees

A portable forest sawmill

When the trees are being planted they are placed $1\frac{1}{2}$ metres apart. This means that 4325 trees are needed for one hectare of land. About 14,000 hectares are planted each year. A multiplication sum will show you that millions of young trees are required.

The work of planting the trees in a forest must be spread over many years. Conifers, which form the bulk of the trees, take at least 70 years to grow to their full size. In order to have a steady supply of fully-grown timber every year, only a section is planted at a time. When the forest is fully planted the oldest trees should be about 20 years older than the youngest trees.

The workers in a forest have many different kinds of work to do. Besides ploughing and planting, they must keep the young trees from weeds for a few years. Harmful insects and rabbits, which eat the bark, must be kept under control. As the trees grow taller the lower branches are cut off to admit more light. When the trees are about fifteen years old they are about 6 metres high. Now is the time for cutting down the weaker trees to leave more growing space for the others. The felled trunks are used as pit props and fencing posts.

Although the trees in a forest have several natural enemies, the greatest enemy of all is fire. In a few hours a forest fire can destroy the results of many years of hard work. If you are picnicking near any wood or forest, never light a fire.

The Forestry Commission employs over 4000 people in Scotland. When the forests are fully planted, it is likely that many more will be needed. This work has made a great difference to many crofters and villagers in the Highlands. Regular work and wages have brought new life to many deserted valleys. New houses have been built for the workers and schools for their children. At the forest of Ae in the Southern Uplands near Dumfries, a whole new village has been built.

One of the Forestry Commission's most interesting projects took place at the Culbin Sands near Nairn on the Moray Firth. In the year 1694 a series of great gales set the high sand dunes on the beach in motion. When the sand stopped moving, a fertile stretch of country, 11 kilometres long and 3 kilometres wide, had become a sandy desert. The mouth of the River Findhorn was blocked, so that it had to find a new outlet to the sea. Farms, houses and churches disappeared completely. For over 200 years the area was a desert.

The foresters' greatest difficulty was to prevent the sand drifting with the wind. Before planting could begin the sand was "thatched" with brushwood of birch and broom, held in place by heavier branches from older plantations. This covering not only prevented the sand moving, but, when it rotted, it provided food for the growing trees. Today at Culbin there is a thriving forest.

Some of the land which the Forestry Commission has bought has not been useful for tree planting. Mountains and moorlands, however, are attractive to those who enjoy hiking, hill climbing, camping and studying nature. Four large areas in Scotland are open to the public as Forest Parks:

1 Argyll Forest Park, between Loch Long and Loch Fyne.

2 Glen Trool Forest Park in Kirkcudbrightshire.

3 Glen More Forest Park in Strathspey, which includes the Cairngorm Mountains and Loch Morlich.

4 Queen Elizabeth Forest Park from the Trossachs to Loch Lomond.

If you visit any of these parks you can wander at will through some of Scotland's finest scenery.

Glenfinart, Argyll Forest Park

74

16 Hydro-electric power

Many boys and girls living in Scotland will have seen the tall, latticed, steel towers, called pylons. Thick copper wires stretched between them carry electricity to towns, villages, and remote crofters' cottages all over the Highlands. Some of this electricity is produced at hydro-electric power stations.

Do you know what is meant by hydro-electricity? Hydro means water, and tells you that the electricity is produced by using the power of falling water.

To create this water power, huge dams have been built across the end of some lochs high in the mountains. Tunnels large enough to hold a double-decker bus are often cut through the mountains to bring more water into the loch. In this way a great volume of water is led to the dam.

From the dam, the water rushes down pipes, wide enough for a man to stand in, to a building called a power house much further down the valley. At the power house the force of the water turns a turbine, which drives a generator, so making electricity. In some places the water passes through two or three power houses before the force of its fall is spent.

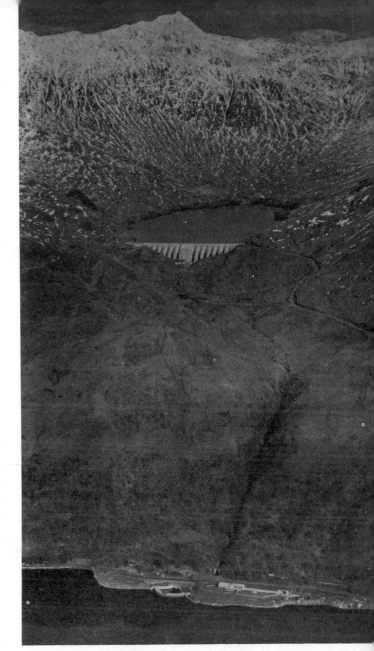

The Ben Cruachan reservoir feeds the hydro-electric station built inside the mountain

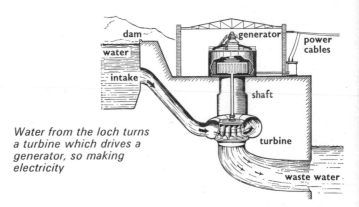

Water from the loch turns a turbine which drives a generator, so making electricity

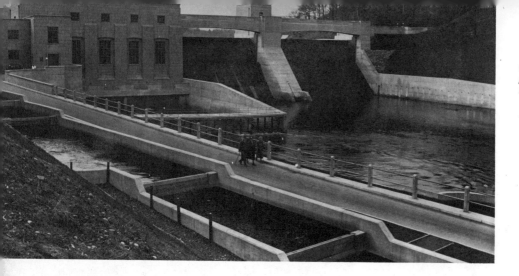

In places where the dam stands across a river, a "fish ladder" is built through the dam to help salmon to get up-stream to spawn. The "ladder" consists of a series of pools rising through the dam. They are connected by under-water pipes through which the fish can pass. At the Pitlochry dam visitors can enter an underground chamber and watch the salmon through a thick glass window. This fish-pass contains thirty-five pools with a rise of about half a metre between each of them.

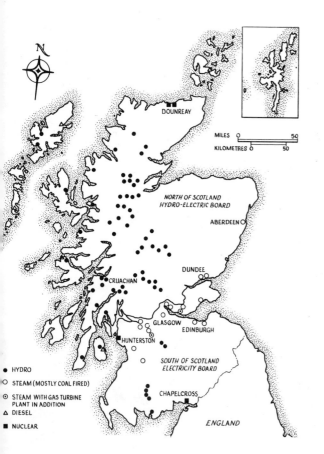

DOUNREAY

MILES 0   50
KILOMETRES 0   50

NORTH OF SCOTLAND
HYDRO-ELECTRIC BOARD

ABERDEEN O

DUNDEE

CRUACHAN

GLASGOW
EDINBURGH

HUNTERSTON

SOUTH OF SCOTLAND
ELECTRICITY BOARD

CHAPELCROSS

ENGLAND

- HYDRO
O STEAM (MOSTLY COAL FIRED)
⊙ STEAM WITH GAS TURBINE
   PLANT IN ADDITION
△ DIESEL
■ NUCLEAR

Most of the dams and power stations have been constructed since 1945. Many millions of units of electricity are produced by water power from the Highland glens. Many schemes are not yet complete, and some have not been started. But when the work is complete, hydro-electricity will be available in nearly every part of the country.

Every year the demand for electric power in homes and industries increases. At the new Hunterston power station on the Ayrshire coast, the steam to drive the turbines comes from atomic power. On the Firth of Forth, the Longannet and Cockenzie power stations use coal from the nearby mines. At Cockenzie 12,000 tonnes are consumed every day. The ash from these two stations is being used to reclaim land from the waters of the Firth.

The production of electricity

Scotland plays Switzerland at Hampden Park, Glasgow

17 The Scots at play

At an early age, boys learn how to play team games. Football is the most popular game, and it is played and watched by thousands of men and boys all over Scotland. Schoolboys often play all the year round, because they so enjoy playing, but professional football is a winter sport, often played under bad weather conditions which are a real test of stamina.

There are many professional clubs, with such famous names as Glasgow Rangers and Celtic. The amateur club Queen's Park has a ground, Hampden Park, which holds 150,000 spectators, and is the largest football enclosure in Britain.

Rugby football, too, is very popular and is played at many Secondary, Grammar and Public Schools throughout the country. The Former Pupils' Clubs from these schools provide most of the teams which play in the senior rugby competition. In the border counties, rugby is much more popular than soccer. Murrayfield in Edinburgh is the ground where international rugby matches are played before crowds of 70,000 spectators. In Scotland, rugby is a completely amateur game, played only during the winter months when the ground is soft.

Other team games popular in Scotland are cricket, in the summer, and hockey and shinty in the colder months. Shinty is similar to ice-hockey, which was derived from it, but there are no rules regulating the height to which a player may raise his stick when striking or stopping the ball.

Playing golf at Gourock

Pony trekking

Curling at Aviemore

No matter where you live in Scotland you are never far from a golf course. Golf started in Scotland hundreds of years ago and is now played in many countries all over the world. The Old Course at St. Andrews, which is a stiff test for the best of players, is known wherever the game is played.

Hill climbing and angling have been popular for many years; pony trekking is a new sport. To go pony trekking you must stay at a hotel or hostel in the Highlands where sturdy highland ponies are kept. The trekking consists of riding the ponies for twenty-five to thirty kilometres each day over the rough hill tracks. Orienteering is a new outdoor activity becoming very popular with members of youth clubs and other organisations for young people.

In winter, when lochs are frozen over, and there is snow on the ground, skating, ski-ing and curling are popular. "The Roarin' Game," as curling is often called, is played mainly in Scotland and in Canada. It is played on ice and is similar to the game of bowls. A curling stone, which is heavy and circular in shape with a flat bottom and a handle on top, is spun across the ice towards a mark.

Let's remember

The land
The mainland of Scotland can be divided into three parts: the Southern Uplands, the Central Lowlands and the Highlands. Less than one-quarter of the land is cultivable. The highest mountains are the Cairngorms and the Grampians; Ben Nevis is the highest peak in Britain. The Clyde and Forth estuaries are the two most important waterways.

Power
Coal is still the chief source of power. The coalfields are in Lanarkshire, Stirling, Fife, Ayrshire and Lothians. Electricity is one of the most convenient forms of power. The huge turbines which produce the electricity can be driven by moving water, by steam from coal-fired furnaces, or by steam from water heated by nuclear fission.

Industries
Shipbuilding and engineering, whose raw materials are coal and iron, are carried on in the Central Lowlands.

Textiles
Jute, linen, cotton thread, woollen cloth and carpets are important textiles made in Scotland.

Agriculture
Think of Ayrshire cows, Aberdeen Angus bulls, Cheviot sheep, poultry, raspberries for jam. Remember that a farmer makes hay and silage, and grows turnips and kail as winter fodder for his animals.

Cities
Edinburgh is the capital of Scotland. It is an important centre for government, banking and insurance. Glasgow is a vast city which produces everything from a packet of sweets to an ocean liner. Aberdeen is often called the Granite City. It is Scotland's chief fishing port. Dundee is the centre of the jute industry.

Universities
There are four ancient universities in Scotland, at St. Andrews, Glasgow, Aberdeen and Edinburgh. The new universities of Strathclyde, Heriot Watt, Dundee and Stirling bring the total to eight.

Exports
One of Scotland's important exports is whisky, which is distilled mainly on Speyside. Scottish tweeds, such as Harris and Cheviot, and high-quality woollen goods, such as jumpers and cardigans, are also exported.

Islands
There are over 700 islands round the coasts, but very few are inhabited. The main island groups are the Outer and Inner Hebrides, the Orkneys and the Shetlands.

Population
Of Scotland's five million people nearly four million live in the Central Lowlands. In the north-west, many of the people from the Highlands and the Islands speak Gaelic amongst themselves.

Index

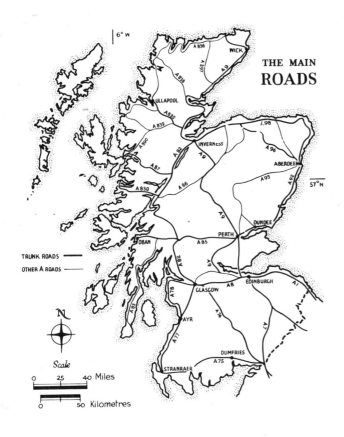

THE MAIN
ROADS

TRUNK ROADS ▬▬▬
OTHER A ROADS ▬▬▬

Scale
0   25   40 Miles
0   50 Kilometres

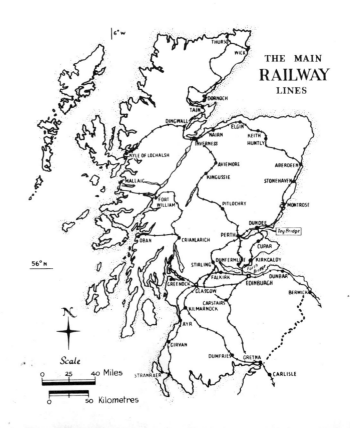

THE MAIN
RAILWAY
LINES

Scale
0   25   40 Miles
0   50 Kilometres